"Gaines is a witty, knowing writer . . . there's rarely a dull page." —Scott Eyman, *Palm Beach Post*

Fool's Paradise: Poseurs, Players and the Culture of Excess in South Beach

"A fun yarn about a bunch of charming scammers and swindlers with garish tastes . . . " —*Miami Herald*

"An entertaining chronicle." —Carl Hiaasen cover of *New York Times Book Review*

"A gossipy social history of scandal and intrigue, Miami Style" —*USA Today*

Obsession; The Lives and Times of Calvin Klein

"Riveting." —*Kirkus Reviews*

"Graphic . . . unflinching . . . vividly told . . . " —*People*

"The hottest book potato of the year." —*Newsweek*

Simply Halston

"The book is filled with wry, witty anecdotes, but it is Halston himself, vividly portrayed by his biographer, who steals the show." —*Booklist*

"Dazzling!" —Liz Smith

"If *Simply Halston* were a movie it would be X-rated." —*The New York Times*

One of
These Things
First

One of These Things First

STEVEN GAINES

Delphinium Books

Harrison, New York • Encino, California

ONE OF THESE THINGS FIRST

First Edition

Jacket and interior design by Jonathan Lippincott

Library of Congress Catalogue-in-Publication Data is available on request.

ISBN 978-1-88-328569-2

16   17   18   19   RRD   10   9   8   7   6   5   4   3   2   1

One of These Things First is a memoir of inexact proportions. Some names,
professions, and locations have been changed to protect the privacy of
living people.

For Muna and Gog

One of
These Things
First

One

Lost Boy

One brilliantly cold afternoon in March of 1962, three months past my fifteenth birthday, I set out on a course of action that would shake my world from its wobbly orbit and spin it off on an unanticipated new trajectory. I managed to escape the hawk-eyed scrutiny of the three saleswomen in whose care I had been left, and slipped behind the brocaded curtain of a fitting room in the back of my grandparents' ladies' clothing store.

The small room was warm and close, the air thick with the cloyingly sweet smell of stale perfume and hairspray. Although only a curtain separated me from the rest of the world, I felt sealed away and safe. Of course, I wouldn't be safe for long because they would soon realize I was missing and come look for me. The saleswomen didn't like me in those fitting rooms. The saleswomen didn't like anything I did. Lily Williams said it wasn't normal for me to go into a fitting room where women got undressed, although one would think it was the most normal thing in the world for a teenage boy to be curious about a place where women were naked. But I guess maybe not those women, who were mostly overweight and middle-aged, with huge pale breasts like kneaded dough, sometimes with nipples stretched as big around as a saucer.

Those were the kind of women who came from all over the five boroughs of New York City to this Mecca of corsetry, to be fitted from the comprehensive stock of sturdy brassieres, girdles, and long-line undergarments, elaborately constructed of elastic and satin, given shape by metal stays covered by pink plush to prevent chafing. Crucial alterations were attended to while-you-wait with the unparalleled expertise of Katherine, my grandfather's chatelaine and sergeant at arms, or by my grandmother, at a black 1955 Singer sewing machine.

There was a period when, aged seven years old, almost every day I ripped open the curtain to one of the fitting rooms to reveal a bewildered, half-naked woman. Thrilled at her mortification, I shouted in my little boy's voice, "Oh! So sorry! I didn't know anybody was in there!" and whipped the curtain closed and ran away. No matter how many times I was punished, I did it again the next day. "Oh! So sorry! I didn't know anybody was in there!"

That day in March 1962 I peeked through the fitting room curtain, one time, two times, and I saw that Lily and Dodie and Fat Anna were all at their stations, facing the other way, lost in their worlds. My mother had gone to pick my father up at school and take him to the accountant to do their taxes, and my grandmother was at the Culver Luncheonette for a coffee-and-English break. Everything was still; there hadn't been a customer in an hour, and the chatter had died into sleepy silence. The only sound was the febrile buzz of the fluorescent lights and the occasional hiss of a radiator. It was sunny outside, but the temperature was in the low teens, and a snowstorm two days before had left dirty drifts piled knee-high along the curb. The sidewalks were coated with ice, and the wind was so strong that people were blown slipping and sliding down the street. Some of the bigger gusts managed to move the heavy glass front door of the store inward an inch, sending up eerie howls of cold air, rushing in like spirits from the street.

Lily Williams was at her usual place, sitting in a bentwood chair midway up between two display cabinets, reading the *World Telegram*. One day when I was hiding in a corrugated box, eavesdropping, I heard Lily say to my grandmother, "Nothing good will come of him being in those fitting rooms." Lily Williams's refrain was that anything I did would come to no good. I would come to no good. It was drummed into me that I had to be nice to the saleswomen, even if they predicted I would come to no good, because they worked for free. They came to be part of Rose's Bras Girdles Sportswear as though they had joined the Foreign Legion, to escape another life, bored and lonely at home. They even wore a kind of uniform—smocks in bright floral prints with patch pockets, purchased at the corner smock and robe store on East 2nd Street, for six dollars each.

I didn't know how Lily Williams knew to tell my grandmother I would come to no good, because she didn't have any children herself, or even nieces and nephews. She was tough old shanty Irish, a weedy, little thing, maybe ninety-five pounds, with a thin face and wavy white hair pinned up behind her head. She earned extra money fabricating flowers out of gossamer petals of silk for a Manhattan milliner. Sometimes she let me help her wire the flowers to their stems. One day, when I was eleven years old, Lily stopped talking to me because I was "fresh" to her. I never realized before that someone could ignore you, as if you didn't exist anymore, even if you spoke to them; they would look the other way or through you.

Dodie Berkowitz was leaning back on the lingerie counter, a string bean with a small belly, chain-smoking Parliaments, holding her cigarettes pointed up in the air like a stick of chalk. She had pretty green eyes, but she was pockmarked, slow to smile, and dour, always tattling on me to Katherine.

My only saleslady friend, Fat Anna, was doing the Crostix behind the sewing machine. She regularly wore the black raiment of an Italian widow, although her husband, a plumber named Angelo, was alive and well. She hugged me with her hammy arms when she saw me, and gave the top of my head a kiss. She said novenas for me at church, and it made me feel important that anyone was praying for me. Fat Anna was the only one who would care. The others would be secretly glad, their faces set in deep satisfaction that they had been right all along—I had come to no good.

I stepped back and considered myself in the mirror. No strapping high school freshman here. I was pale and pudgy, and I had tortured my mess of wavy strawberry blond hair into a perfect inch-high pompadour, hardened in place with thick white hair cream, like plaster of Paris. I had meticulously doctored an inflamed whitehead under my bottom lip with Clearasil, so I wouldn't be embarrassed when they found me. I was also spiffed up for the occasion, new clothes, slacks and sweater in shades of forest green, the big retail color of the season.

I moved closer to my reflection until my breath condensed on the glass and I tasted it with my tongue, one lick, two licks, cold and salty, and I concentrated deeply into the eyes of the boy in the mirror and tried to will another boy out of me, like the spirits that stepped out of dead bodies in the movies, only this boy would tell me if I could grow up, or maybe it was the boy who was pushing the lawnmower in Lynbrook who would grow up for me. Maybe I had the whole thing backwards, maybe I should go *into* the mirror, and then I would be him.

But when I put my forehead up against the glass to see if I could pass through the surface, it was hard and unyielding, so I just stood there with my head pressed against it, staring at myself until my face began to decompose into a black-and-white pointillist mask, and I liked that, so I stared some more, the blood pounding in my head. Then I remembered that I had to get on with what I was doing.

With the three women preoccupied, I slipped out from behind the dressing room curtain like a cat burglar and through a paneled door a few feet away. It opened into a crescent-shaped stockroom, carved out of the leftover space behind the shelves in the store. It was dank and smelled like wet dog. Years ago my grandparents kept two mutts, Patsy and Toddy, back there as watchdogs—the poor dogs had to live in such a small space, and the room had never stopped smelling of wet dog. On one side were an unkempt toilet and a tiny sink with rusted faucets that ran only cold water. The walls were lined floor to ceiling with shelves of Goldstar hosiery in thin boxes and gold wrapping. Inside each box was a pair of hose in one of the combinations of sizes and colors and styles (size 6/Smokey taupe/seamless/no heel), wrapped around a cardboard form. There were no credit cards back then, everything was cash, and I knew that on some nights my grandfather didn't make a bank deposit and hid thousands of dollars in cash in some of those boxes, stashed among the others in a special position on the shelf that only he and Katherine could decipher.

Hiding the money in a complicated pattern was just part of the preventive measures and fortifications my grandfather had devised against what seemed be an imminent robbery. There had already been a terrible incident in his house on Long Island. Two robbers—let into the house during the day by the washing machine repairman, the police detective later surmised, although unprovable—hid in the house all day waiting for my grandparents and Katherine to come home. One waited in the attic (the police found sandwich wrappers and cigarette butts), the other sat behind the curve in the sectional sofa (more sandwich wrappers), crouching right behind them while they watched Jack Paar before going to bed.

And when my grandparents and Katherine went to sleep, the robbers injected something into the air conditioning unit—my grandfather found a slit cut in the duct fabric in the basement—and the split-level house filled with a sleeping gas that put them in a stupor. Katherine remembered being in a dream state, while the robbers rolled her aside to look under her mattress for her *knipple*, a Jewish woman's secret stash of money. The police said that if a child (like me) had been staying in the house, the sleeping gas would have killed him. The house was ransacked, and all the cash receipts from the Friday and Saturday of Mother's Day weekend, nearly $20,000, were gone.

The store's rear door was made of steel, and it hung on

enormous iron hinges, with a twenty-five-pound crossbar in hasps holding it shut. I touched it one time, two times, and with some effort lifted it out of its metal brackets and leaned it against the wall. Then I touched the door one time, two times, and tugged mightily on the door ring until the door opened a few inches with a high-pitched squeak. I inched it back one time, two times, and again until it was open as far as I could get it to go, about four feet, revealing another door, the original wood door of the building, with peeling green paint and four dirty window-panes of beveled glass. Through the windows I could see a patch of the dirt backyard, no more than ten feet square, closed in by the cinder-block rear walls of the garages on Parkville Avenue behind us.

Now I began to work quickly. I took off my forest-green wool sweater, folded it the way I had been taught to fold merchandise, equal number of folds on each side, and laid it carefully on an unopened carton against the wall. Then I rolled back the sleeves of my tartan plaid flannel shirt in three-inch folds, one time, two times on the right, one time, two times on the left, making sure the sides matched, and I turned resolutely toward the door. Like a conductor about to give the orchestra a downbeat, I raised my clenched fists and then with all my might I punched through the two lower windowpanes of glass, one fist through each, one fist, two fists, except I ruined it because I had to punch the left one twice to get my fist through it. I sawed my wrists and forearms twice back and forth across the shards that held in the frame.

At first I hardly felt anything at all, and for a second I thought maybe I was already dead, and then *foof* the pain walloped me and I did wish I was dead. My whole body contracted in a spasm of shock. Why didn't I think about *this* part? Stupid not to think about this part, but too late now. God please take my fucking arms off. Lop them right off and cauterize the stumps, just make it stop. I looked down to see what kind of damage I had done. There was especially vicious harm to my left wrist and forearm, where the shards had filleted open the flesh like a white fish, and the wound was pulsating bright red blood. That was a fatal rupture, I realized. Was it the artery that took the blood away or sent it to—where? I pressed my left arm against my belly and with my right hand I managed to unhook the rickety door and I stepped out into the backyard.

The air was icy, it was arctic. A half a block away on the elevated line the Coney Island D train crashed by, showering McDonald Avenue in silver sparks. I could hear Ottalie Kantor practicing *Malaguena* on the piano on Parkville Avenue. She had come to the part toward the end where it gets really spirited, and the music swirled into my mind and I was dancing dying. Clammy and suddenly drowsy, I lay down on the frozen dirt next to the rosebush, where the previous summer I had gathered thorny American Beauties for my grandmother, and I waited to bleed out.

I hadn't been missing more than five minutes before Dodie noticed and Lily went looking for me and she saw the door open in the back room and me asleep on the ground lying in what she said looked like melted chocolate. Out the door and down the street she ran in her smock to the Culver Luncheonette and screamed for my grandmother to come. I hoped Arnie and Irv behind the counter were happy. The fairy is dying.

It was just then that my grandfather pulled his pearlized blue Cadillac Biarritz into a parking space in front of Fleischman's, and he and Katherine saw Lily and my grandmother running down the icy street, my grandmother's face ashen. He followed them into the store and out to the backyard, where my grandmother's high-pitched wails penetrated even my numbing sleep.

"My, my, my," my grandfather said softly, calmly, kneeling down in the garden to get a better look at me. My blood soaked the knees of his pants. When he saw my arms he cried, "Why, my sweet child?" But he wasn't really asking a question. I looked up at him with glassy eyes. He was young for a grandfather, only fifty-eight years old. He had green-blue eyes and a long, narrow nose. I didn't think he was handsome, but I understood why women loved him so. My eyes rolled up and he whistled long and low in amazement. I hoped that he wouldn't be angry with me, even for this, but it didn't occur to me that I was doing something to him as well as me.

Then the harpies were behind him, sending up a chorus of caterwauls, turning into bats with bat faces as they peered down at me over his shoulder, come to no good. I couldn't motion them, punch them away, because I was in one of those grainy foreign movies that came on TV very late at night, where there are long pauses and everything seems still. It hardly hurt anymore anyway. My grandfather wrapped towels around my wrists and arms and tried to scoop me up but I was too big to lift, so he began to cry more and shouted for them to call the police. Then there was more commotion and more wailing, and later they said my grandmother was standing in the middle of 18th Avenue screaming. When the police arrived they didn't have a stretcher, but they said not to wait—in those days it could take fifteen minutes for an ambulance to come—so they shifted me onto a rough woolen blanket and carried me out to the police cruiser, where they laid me down in the backseat with my head on my grandfather's lap. I could feel the seam of the blanket under my finger, getting wet with my blood. I touched it once, touched it twice.

One of the policemen in the front seat turned around and said to me, "Hey pal, you a Dodger fan?" and when I didn't answer he said, "Why'd you do something like that?"

They took me to Brooklyn Doctor's Hospital, a grim place that looked more like a small brick apartment building than a hospital. It was the same place where my mother had her gallbladder out, and where my father's father was taken when he had his heart attack, and where I was born fifteen years and three months before, about twenty minutes before midnight in late November 1946, after my mother endured twenty-seven hours in a labor so brutal that she swore she would never have another child, and she didn't.

"Did you do this to yourself?" a man in a white coat asked me loudly, as if I was deaf. "Or did somebody do this to you?" I felt pinpricks and *whoosh* I was numb all over. I vomited, probably the wonton soup from the Great World that I had chosen as my last meal, so they cleared my throat and then something shifted, I felt different, very light, slipping, and the bus came by and I jumped on it just as graceful as Gene Kelly hopping on a trolley. I slid into comforting nothingness, out of reach in the dark except for an annoying metallic sound that sounded something like "Stay with us." One time, two times, gone.

Brooklyn

Oh Brooklyn, my Brooklyn. Life could offer no richer lesson than to simply grow up there. I wouldn't have had it any other way, not for any suburban childhood or silver-spoon, Upper East Side private school education. Brooklyn. I even loved the way the name sounded, *Brooue-keh-len*, a Dutch word, meaning "fractured lands," some say, and also the name of a medieval village of not much interest in Utrecht, in the middle of the Netherlands. But none of us knew that, and nobody cared anyway. We were at the center of our own universe.

Brooklyn was the *emes*, the authentic thing. They made fun of people from Brooklyn on TV and in the movies—you know, it was always pudgy William Bendix who was from Brooklyn, a stand-up guy but none too smart, or a dumb blond with a good heart who chewed gum and said, "toidy-toid-and-toid." But what they missed was Brooklyn's noble soul. We were the salt of the earth, two million strong, almost all of us immigrants or the children of immigrants. Brooklyn had grown from the stub of Long Island farmland to a bunch of close-knit neighborhoods, New World *shtetels* and parishes, rooted by family, faith, and country. When you talked about the heart of America, it was *us* as much as Kansas. We were the real melting pot. We had Italians, Jews, and Irish living in equal and surprisingly harmonious distribution. I was only once called a "Christ killer," when I was ten years old, by a kid in my class whom my mother dismissed as a "juvenile delinquent."

We lived in Borough Park, the cognac of Brooklyn, the potent and flavorful essence, a neighborhood of low commercial buildings and retail shops, two-family row houses made of brick and stucco, here and there a six-story red brick apartment building. It was nowhere in the middle of nowhere, but it was alive with dreams. There were churches on every corner—it was called "the borough of churches"—and synagogues by the thousands, and candy stores by the millions. There wasn't much crime, no matter how prepared my grandfather was, no stickups or bank robberies, no purse snatchers in the street. The most dishonest people I knew were the gypsy women who shoplifted from the *What One Dollar!* rack that stood on the terrazzo marble of the store's vestibule in the summer months.

I could spend weeks without leaving the block I lived on. Eighteenth Avenue was my world, complete as far as I was concerned. I knew every one of the 182 concrete squares on our sidewalk. There, where I fell and cracked my head open trying to learn to ride a two-wheeler. There, where before I was born, a dog had stepped into the wet cement and left four perfect paw impressions, a canine fingerprint. And over there, where Uncle Saul hoisted me in his arms when I was four years old to see the silver spaceship float across the sky, or at the curb opposite the store, where an indomitable clump of weeds grew from a crevice of black dirt, my only flora, for there were no trees on this block in Brooklyn.

Our block was the Borough Park bus and truck company of Grover's Corners, with our own characters and plot twists. Would Mr. Fleischman, a haughty German Jew who wore a pocket handkerchief and owned the gown shop down the block, have a second heart attack? Would Old Man McGlynn drink himself to death in his dark saloon, McGlynn's Inn, where he and other scary men sat in shadows, hunched over the bar all day? Would Sima, the lovely young woman with hearing aids who lived above Klenetsky's kosher butcher and made papier-mâché marionettes for the neighborhood children, ever get past her deafness and find love and have children of her own? Did jolly Mr. Silverstein, of Silverstein's Fine Delicatessen, with the best stuffed breast of veal in all of Brooklyn, know his son, who lived in Los Angeles, was a pornographer? Was it true that the window display of Schecter's Smock Shop hadn't changed in fifteen years, and no one had noticed?

Did the disabled vet who owned the candy store with a rack of comic books have a funny walk because he lost his testicles during the war? And what secrets did Nate Berkowitz have, whose hand once brushed against Katherine's leg, she claimed, sitting next to him at the Culver Luncheonette? Every day Berkowitz stood just inside the front door of his linoleum-and-carpet store, chain-smoking Tareytons, a horse-track betting sheet stuck in his back pocket, a fedora hiding his yarmulke so as not to put off *goyim* customers.

Who was the mentally handicapped man who appeared on the corner near the stairs to the elevated line every afternoon at five o'clock, and sang in a high falsetto to the tune of "La donna è mobile," *My name is Hen-er-ry, I live in Coney Island, put me on the D train, the money's in my pocket*? What about the man who was waiting for a train at the 18th Avenue stop of the elevated line and had to take a pee, and when he peed on the third rail the electricity ran up his urine and electrocuted him through his penis?

And what about the Culver Theater?

Well, it was glorious, and it was mine. It was cavernous, nearly fifteen hundred seats, an ornate relic of the 1920s.

It had a dramatic ceiling mural of figures in white gauzy gowns in a sort of daisy chain, and every form of seraphim and cherubim that the imagination could summon was pictured holding up the faux columns along the walls. The theater was also equipped with a Wurlitzer 2 manual, 7 rank organ so powerful it could vibrate the seats and make sound effects like horses' hooves and a steamboat whistle to accompany silent films, but it was long ago turned off. Also long gone was a Chinese garden and outdoor screening area, where in the summer you could watch movies and sip lemonade under the Brooklyn moon. When I was a child they hung a white satin "Air Cooled" banner with blue fringe from the marquee in the summer, and if you stood by the theater when the lobby doors swung open for a half a second you were enveloped by a blast of popcorn-scented Freon.

By the 1950s the Culver hadn't screened a first-run movie in twenty years. It sometimes took months for a picture that opened in Manhattan to trickle down to us. A big hit, like *King Kong*, could take a year. The theater stayed alive with a kids' double feature every Saturday at noon along with twenty-five cartoons that often drew a thousand rowdy neighborhood kids. My mom and dad and I went to the Friday night promotions when the new movies were put in and collected pieces of the free eight-piece place setting in a modern pattern. Over the years we assembled hundreds of pieces of mismatched cheap china from which we ate.

My grandmother was chums with Murray-the-manager. Muna—I called her that instead of "grandma"—gave Murray's wife free hosiery—the wife had diabetes—and somehow Murray rigged it so that at one Saturday afternoon matinee I won a Schwinn two-wheel bicycle in a raffle promotion the theater was holding. Murray also let me in without paying, whenever I wanted. During the week in the afternoon the theater was almost always empty, and I had the place to myself. I went to the movies like other kids turned on the TV set. Oh the places I went, the people I met, the things I saw from the fifth row on the left aisle, where my mother made me sit so she could always find me, and pressed fifty cents into the hands of one of the tough matrons to keep me safe.

Cheek by jowl with the Culver Theater was the IND elevated line, which made its presence known in the theater with a rumble every ten minutes or so, the trains thundering by only twenty feet from the theater wall. The El, which dissected 18th Avenue at the corner, blocked our afternoon sun and kept McDonald Avenue directly below it in shadows. It was a rudimentary two-story structure of beams and braces, like a child's Erector Set, caked with city grime and held together with rivets the size of a man's fist. The station platform was completely open, no fences or walls, and I loved going up there, the trains blowing my hair as they blasted by, the Culver Theater's big wraparound marquee of a hundred clear lightbulbs just beyond my reach. It was like a crane shot in a movie where the camera pulls back, revealing an Edward Hopper tableau come to life. I stood on the station platform transfixed for hours watching our little drama unfold below, the people going about their business, the big store in the middle of the block with the pink neon *Rose's Bras Girdles Sportswear* sign, the salesgirls and customers and shopkeepers, my father's frightening rages, the tragic secret of my perversion, my

grandfather's shameful affairs, all this marked in quarter
tones by the roar of the passing trains.

Lawnmower Boy

Funny thing was, although the D train right on the corner connected us easily with Manhattan, we went there
only for special occasions, like going to see a Broadway
show for a birthday or to eat at a famous restaurant like
Mama Leone's or Luchow's. Otherwise Brooklyn had everything we needed or wanted, all of it happily lacking
in the complications of "the city." They called Brooklyn
"Manhattan's bedroom," because so many of the people
who worked there during the day went home to Brooklyn
on the train at night. So Brooklyn wasn't exactly provin-
cial, but I'd guess that most people in Borough Park in
the 1950s and 1960s, when I was growing up, didn't know
much about, say, international diplomacy, or fine wines, or
haute couture. Or psychiatry. Or homosexuals.

Well, there was one homo I knew, to use the *lingua
franca* of Brooklyn in the 1950s. He was a freak, nature's
mistake, like in a science fiction movie where a man melds
with a woman, a creature that didn't deserve to live. It terrified me just to be in his presence. He rented the basement apartment at Aunt Gertie's house on Avenue F, and
sometimes at big family dinners he helped serve and clean
up for five dollars and I got to look at him, but I avoided
making eye contact. I figured he knew about me. All nature's mistakes recognize each other. Michelle, as they
called him—he let them call him that (his name was Michael but he seemed to think it was okay to call him Mi-

chelle)—had manicured nails and plucked eyebrows and he walked like a girl. Once he said he watched wrestling on TV when he folded the laundry, and my father called him a fairy and a homo behind his back. And there was one other homo I heard of, Christine Jorgensen. My parents and Big Rich and Tina were joking about it one night, smoking cigarettes and drinking coffee in Tina's kitchen. They said that Christine Jorgensen was a homo who went to Sweden and had his dick and balls cut off.

I didn't want to have my dick and balls cut off. So I kept it a secret that I was a homo as best I could, and I watched how other boys moved and walked and talked, and I tried to look and be like them. But I guess it was already showing, after what Arnie and Irving said a month before I tried to kill myself.

Arnie and Irv, I had known them my whole life. They were okay guys, I looked up to them. They owned the Culver Luncheonette, nestled into the side of the Culver Theater, and I was in there every day. We all were. The whole neighborhood was in and out of that place all day. It was just five doors down from the store, and the salesgirls went there for coffee and an English muffin. The soda fountain had large plate glass windows facing the street, and everybody sitting on one of the twelve stools at the long counter could watch what was happening on street, like watching a movie on a Cinemascope screen. I must have eaten a million cheeseburgers sitting at the counter, absently staring out the big window at the world going by, while my grandmother Rose had her afternoon English and coffee, and kibitzed with Arnie and Irv and the other customers.

The whole neighborhood knew Rose, who owned the

bra and girdle shop. She was a neighborhood luminary. She was barely five feet tall, honey blond, with hair teased like cotton candy sprayed with shellac. Her jokes were corny, but she kept them coming. She had her following too. Customers dropped into the store just to say hello. She always had some cheering advice, usually, "This too shall pass," and a few stories. She could be touchingly sweet, even as she told dirty jokes. Every day she wore the same immaculate outfit—a blouse, a skirt, white nurse's shoes, and a freshly pressed, spotless smock with a folded, clean handkerchief in her pocket she often used to dry my tears.

One afternoon at the Culver Luncheonette I was sitting with her at the counter, savoring an onion bialy with butter and tangy American cheese, along with a tall glass of ice-cold chocolate milk made from U-Bet syrup. It was so good I absently whistled. Twice.

Arnie, balding, doughy, in an apron behind the counter, called to his partner, "Hey, Irving! What whistles besides birds and fairies?"

So I took a big sip of chocolate milk, one time, two times, as if I didn't hear what was just said, and I pretended that sipping the delicious, cold, thick chocolate milk was all that mattered in the world. It was a stupid joke because people whistle, birds chirp and sing, and who knows what fairies do? But I got the point. They just said it, out of the clear blue, with immunity. I guess you have to hate a child to say something like that. I dared not look at Arnie and Irving because acknowledging them with even a glance would make me complicit in their taunt, but I couldn't stop myself, and when I peeked they were both snickering.

My grandmother got very quiet. She looked deeply aggravated. I knew she would have stuck up for me except that calling attention to it would probably only make it worse. Anyway, she wasn't much for confrontation. So we stared straight ahead out the window, one bite, two bites, and then Muna frostily asked for a check. At the cash register she raised herself to her full five feet and said to Irv, "I'll never come back here again. *Never.*"

But she started going back in a week. You couldn't blame her; it was the only place to get an English.

From then on, every time I walked past the big glass windows of the Culver Luncheonette, Arnie and Irving minced around inside and curtsied to me like a girl. I prayed they would get tired of it, but it continued to amuse them. I considered telling my father, but I was too ashamed. What could I say—they tease me for being a homo? And then what would he do? Storm the ramparts of the luncheonette to complain that his son was being mocked for being a *fegele*? I had to stop walking past the luncheonette altogether. I began to cross to the other side of the street, and I walked with my face turned away, toward the wall. Even when I went to the Culver Theater, which was right next door to the luncheonette, I walked all the way around the block to get there.

If Arnie and Irving could tell, I suppose everybody knew. I promised myself that I would make it untrue. I promised myself that I would not let myself think homo thoughts, yet I could think of nothing else. I was haywire with hormones. I spent most of the time walking around in a semi-hunch, trying to hide an erection that wouldn't subside, desperate to find a place to jerk off, mind-wrestling to keep my thoughts away from rubbing my chest against the chest of another boy, which was as far as my stifled sexual expression had progressed. "Chest to chest," I thought of it. "Let's go chest to chest," I would whisper to the lawn-mower boy as we embraced and melted.

The lawnmower boy was a deity in whom I invested all my yearnings. I glimpsed him one Sunday out of the car window from behind the Franconia Notch decal, as my father was driving us randomly around the Five Towns, Long Island's repository of new-money, second-generation Jews in the 1960s. We spent many weekends gawking at the spoils of postwar, split-level prosperity on Long Island and became connoisseurs of model homes. We strolled through scores of them over the years, oohing and aahing over fireplaces and in-wall ovens, debating the virtues and deficits of the layouts and landscaping, then got back in the car, sighed, and drove off to another house we would never be able to afford.

My dad was proud to have his master's in education from New York University and to be a tenured teacher and guidance counselor with the New York City Board of Education, but teachers made lousy money back then, and even though he held down a second job teaching at night school in Manhattan, we were always scrimping to get by. One year my mother stuffed envelopes for a mail-order business for two cents each so we could pay installments on our living room furniture. My dad knew he'd never be able to buy us one of those houses in Hewlett Bay Harbor, or Lawrence, or a house like my grandfather, Gog, had in Freeport, with its two-car garage and celebrity bandleader who lived next door. Still, we dreamed and drove.

The Lawnmower Boy was mowing the lawn of a house in a development in Lynbrook. I saw him fleetingly, no more than a slow camera pan as he passed in and out of frame, but I knew him so intimately from that moment that

I can still smell the sun on the nape of his neck. He was bare-chested, his white tee shirt hanging out of the back pocket of his blue jeans, and his black high-top sneakers were unlaced. He was a real boy, not a fake boy like me, and everything about him was normal—the peach fuzz above his upper lip, eyebrows bleached blond from the sun, brown nipples the size of dimes, an electrifying trail of dark hair that began at his navel and disappeared into the elastic band of his Fruit of the Loom underwear. Chest to chest with me.

He was with me every day after that, the ectoplasm of my desire. I called him Nathaniel when we talked, but in my mind, like God, he had no name. When I didn't pay attention to him, he jealously intruded into my thoughts and made me hard. He was a show-off. Mischievous and endlessly entertaining. I masturbated thinking about going chest to chest with him half a dozen times a day, and every time I finished I was so filled with remorse and shame that I would beat my head with my fists until there were red bumps across my forehead. I would swear to *Adonai* that I would banish him, but I didn't know how to make him go away, and anyway, I really didn't want him to.

Rifka

The only person crazier than me that I knew growing up was my grandfather's older sister, Aunt Rifka.

Rifka was a big-boned woman with a hook nose and bosoms that swayed in her full slip like cannonballs in a sling. She was a gentle soul, guileless and loving. Her silver hair was tied into a messy braid that she wound up and pinned at the back of her head, like a charwoman. The great joy of her life was her sixteen-year-old, titian-haired daughter, Becky, a teenage piano prodigy who made her public debut at Carnegie Hall as part of a roster of talented student musicians from the five boroughs. She played Rifka's favorite that afternoon, Beethoven's haunting *Für Elise*. Three weeks later Becky's joints turned black-and-blue. Leukemia. It was 1944 and they didn't know how to treat it. In a month she was dead. That fast. Rifka, unable to process what had happened, fell apart. Almost overnight her eyes sank deep into her face, the sockets outlining her skull, and she entered an alternate reality in which Becky was alive. When Rifka returned home from the cemetery, she set a place at the big dining room table for her, and served a plate of food to the empty chair.

Her family indulged her changing Becky's sheets and calling Becky's alarmed piano teacher to resume Becky's lessons, but when Rifka began to hold conversations—and sometimes argue—with Becky, they committed her to Creedmoor Psychiatric Center in Queens, New York, a Five Boroughs version of Bedlam. At Creedmoor they gave Rifka a course of shock treatments, and then another course, and then a third, and when she came home she was so fried she hardly remembered anything at all, let alone Becky. She absentmindedly began to dress in a full slip and kitchen apron, with flesh-colored support hose that wrinkled at her ankles like folds of skin, her thin legs swallowed up by her huge black shoes.

Rifka and her husband Shmuel, an immigrant house-painter she met at a July 4th parade in Prospect Park, already had hard luck with their first child—the lumbering giant Seymour, who was born with six fingers on each hand and six toes on each foot, as well as undescended testicles. Doctors removed the extra digits on his hands, but they left the extra toes on his feet so he would have better balance when he walked, causing him to wear giant shoes that looked like racquetball paddles. His testicles were surgically lowered into his empty ball sac, but I didn't even want to think about that.

Poor cousin Seymour was also "slow," as everyone delicately put it, a little impaired, or maybe just stupid, but he was also irascible, lazy, and eager for his rich Uncle Harry, my grandfather, to drop dead, because Seymour assumed he would be left a great deal of money. Seymour referred to my grandfather's death as "when my ship comes in."

Slow or not, the Jewish imperative was marriage, so one day Rifka, dressed in finery she wore only if she was going to visit some potentate, and went to the Manhattan offices on West 34th Street of Mr. Field, the famous Jewish matchmaker, for a consultation. Mr. Field, a small man dwarfed by the large leather chair in which he sat, told Rifka that for $1,500 he could introduce Seymour to a woman named Esther, who was also slow, and whose father owned a bakery in Canarsie. If Esther and Seymour were a match, part of her dowry would be that Seymour would be taught how to bake bagels and bialys at her father's bakery, and he would have a trade to support his wife. On the occasion of their wedding, Mr. Field would be paid a second $1,500.

On Seymour and Esther's first date they went to the movies on Kings Highway and held hands in the dark. On their second date Seymour proposed marriage on the E train to Sheepshead Bay, where they spent the afternoon looking at model apartments to rent. A rental agent, who momentarily left them alone in the empty bedroom of one of the model apartments, returned to find the couple lying on floor of the walk-in closet, fully clothed, kissing passionately. The agent, unaware that this was a poignant moment—probably the first and only moment of ardor in the couple's lives—threatened to call the police, which terrified them, and she threw them out.

That night when Esther returned home, buoyant with her marriage proposal, she naively told her parents of the brief romantic passage on the walk-in closet floor. The parents were horrified, and Seymour was banished. Mr. Field branded him a letch and refused to give Aunt Rifka her money back. Seymour's heart was broken. He pined for Esther the rest of his time on earth, lying in bed in his mother's house, listening to sports on the radio. He died at age fifty-eight, a bachelor.

I knew all this because when I was in the sixth grade, Aunt Rifka's two-family house on East 47th Street was right across the street from the schoolyard of PS 192. For all of sixth grade I went to Rifka's house twice a day, the first visit at lunchtime, when she made me huge meals served in a soup bowl: overflowing tunafish sandwiches on toasted white bread with a whopping side of mashed potatoes and butter. The second visit was after school let out. The other kids would scatter into the school yard, a Martian landscape to me, while I went to Aunt Rifka's living room and practiced piano for an hour on the piano on which dead Becky had practiced. Aunt Rifka requested I played *Für Elise* several times every afternoon, while poor lumbering Cousin Seymour would lie in bed in his room listening. Sometimes I repeated the first two expectant notes of the piece, stretching them out until the tone was only a lingering vibration in an unbearable repetition, and I could hear Seymour moan loudly in his room, "I can't stand to hear it anymore."

One day when I was on my way to Aunt Rifka's, a neighborhood boy whose mother shopped in my grandparents' store asked me where I went every day after school. I debated telling him that my father didn't like me to go to the schoolyard because he was afraid I'd get hurt, and that when my father was a little boy another kid in the school yard kicked him in the balls and he had a "rupture," and the doctors had to put lamb tendons in his groin. Instead I told him I had to go to my Aunt Rifka's house to practice piano. He seemed a bit flustered. "Do you like that?" he asked.

"I can play *Für Elise* from beginning to end," I told him.

He looked confused. "Well, Liberace is laughing all the way to the bank," he said cheerfully.

I shrugged like I didn't understand what he meant, but I did, and I walked across the street.

White Rabbit

The summer I was ten years old I was all angles and bones, like a stick figure in khaki shorts and a Camp Lokanda tee shirt, such a skinny-marink that they gave me peanut-butter-and-jelly sandwiches before bed to fatten me up. A coed, kosher camp, Lokanda was the stuff of childhood dreams: sun-dappled white bunkhouses with maroon shutters, towering Adirondack pine forests, meadows of wildflowers, archery, horseback riding, nature walks through the woods, and the crystal-clear, bracing waters of Loch Ada to swim in. My bunkhouse leaked in three places when it rained, and bats slept in the eaves and fluttered through the air at night like butterflies. I was in heaven.

The eight kids in my bunkhouse all had their B-movie roles: Squeaky, the runt mascot; Fetsy (Yiddish for "fart"), the pudgy kid with horn-rimmed glasses; Moe, the goofy kid with a sad smile who could outrun even Brucie Cohen; and Brucie Cohen, our leader, child Adonis, the athletic kid with a stubby crew cut and dismissive glare, for whom I developed strange, unsettling feelings. And there was freckled me, the liability exiled to deep center field, waiting for a long drive that never came, just me and the grasshoppers in the hot sun. In a world where status and popularity were based on brute athletic prowess, I could not name one player for the Brooklyn Dodgers, but I knew the style number to three different kinds of White Swan panties.

One afternoon, during a softball game, I lay down in the sweet meadow grass to watch the clouds pass overhead, and I closed my eyes and fell asleep. When I woke the sun was low over Loch Ada, the game was long over, and my bunkmates had gone to get ready for dinner without noticing I was missing. Instead of being upset, I lay back down in the grass and looked up at the sky and it dawned on me that no one in the world knew where I was. I was in no one's thoughts. I was a secret. For that moment I didn't exist. I had an erection, and I rubbed myself through my shorts and thought about Brucie Cohen's chest, and a spasm went through me. I was ashamed of what I had just done, mortified about what I had been thinking. And continued to think. Could not stop thinking. I had to turn away when Brucie Cohen was near me, and one time tears ran down my cheeks I was so upset by my desire to kiss him.

I felt a different kind of gnawing need another day. I was walking with my bunkmates down a grassy path from the dining hall when I saw a gooey ice cream stick, covered with scurrying ants, lying at the side of the trail. The thought came into my head—it wasn't so much a thought as a feeling—that the stick was lonely and I had to pick it up and take it with me. An uncomfortable electric tingling sensation that I had never felt before filled my chest. I thought if I didn't pick up the stick, it would be lonely for the rest of its life. It had no life, it was a stick. Yet it would be intolerably lonely if I didn't rescue it. I could *feel* the loneliness in the stick, and if you suggested that perhaps I was the one who was lonely, I might have agreed. But that wouldn't have stopped me from having to pick up the stick. Nothing could stop me from picking up that stick. There was no longer any reason why, there was only the need to get the stick and make the unbearable feeling stop.

So I broke away from my bunkmates and snatched the pop stick from the ground, ants and all, and stuck it in the right pocket of my khaki shorts. When I caught up with my fellow campers, one of them asked what I had gone back for, so I said, "Dropped a penny."

After that, I was terrified to look at anything lest I needed to keep it. Out of nowhere compulsion tyrannized me. Some of it led to no small feats of pilfering: it's not easy to spirit away a catcher's mask from a softball game. Within a few weeks, hidden in my footlocker were a whisk broom, Brucie Cohen's sock I took from the washing machine, assorted pebbles and stones, a *Famous Monsters of Filmland* magazine that belonged to a kid in another bunk, my counselor's toothpaste tube, a toilet paper roll, a butterfly under glass from the nature shack, knives and forks, pennies, chewed bubble gum, a sliver of soap from a garbage pail in the shower room, and a prayer book from Saturday morning services.

I tried desperately to figure out what was happening. Was I putting these thoughts into my head purposely or did they appear randomly? Maybe an alien had taken over my body, like in *It Came from Outer Space*, a really spooky science fiction movie in which people in an Arizona town looked like themselves, but an alien controlled their thoughts. Could there be an alien inside my brain? I seriously considered it.

Or was this what it felt like to be crazy? Could you even *be* crazy at my age? I was ten. Rhoda Penmark, the child serial killer in *The Bad Seed*, for which Patty McCormack was nominated as best supporting actress, was crazy, and she was my age. So it was possible I was losing my mind.

On the day I stole the prayer book after services I became so distraught that I ran a fever and vomited. The camp nurse put me in the infirmary, a little white cottage that smelled of alcohol, away from the rest of the bunks. The camp owners, "Uncle" Sammy and "Aunt" Ellie, phoned my parents to say that they were worried about me. When I spoke to my mom and dad on the phone I begged them to come and get me. For a second I thought about saying, "I need to take things . . . ," but my father was on the extension, and Uncle Sam and Aunt Ellie were standing nearby listening, so I said the lame thing that I began to say over and over through the years when I was at a loss to explain

the confusion in my head: "I don't feel well." Not very evoc-
ative or compelling. "I just don't *feel* well."

The following day my parents made the three-hour
drive to Glen Spey and my father let my mother have it in
the car the whole way. He could really go at her: she was
a fat slob, her father was a whoremaster, and he was having a heart attack and/or going to kill himself. By the time
they arrived at Camp Lokanda she had such a bad migraine
she could hardly see. I ran to her and hugged her, a mist of
Arpège perfume calming me like nepenthe, while my dad
stood back and puffed out his cheeks, grumbling about my
"pulling this shit" and repeatedly calling me "Mister."

We went to my bunkhouse and while he waited outside, smoking cigarettes, my mother and I packed my
belongings—all my Camp Lokanda clothing into which
she had just weeks before sewn name tags. I saw the look
on her face when she discovered the items in the bottom
of my footlocker. She knew instantly I had taken them,
stolen them, but she didn't ask, "What are these doing
here?" Instead she looked at me wide-eyed and packed
my clothes on top of my stash so no one would see it, an
act of complicity for which I was grateful.

At that moment cheers of excitement rose up outside.
We could hear laughter and whoops of pleasure. Gracie,
the camp's pet white rabbit, had gotten loose from her
cage and run away from the nature shack. The whole
camp was trying to capture her. I ran down the steps of
my bunkhouse and got caught up in the pursuit along with
dozens of kids. We chased the rabbit in circles in and out
and around the cabins, all of us shouting and laughing, and
after a few exhilarating minutes, the rabbit ran right toward me and stopped. Just like that. She sat twitching her

nose in front of me, like a dog that had come to its master. She looked up at me with little black marble eyes and held my gaze. I thought *this rabbit knows that I'm crazy*. I approached her slowly and she allowed me to lean over and pick her up in my arms, where she nestled calmly. There were cheers from the other campers. They all surrounded me and I was a celebrity. It was thrilling. The nature counselor took the rabbit from me and an older boy patted me on the back and said "Good job!" and then my parents came and got me because my camp trunk was in the car, and it was a long drive, and we had to go. I told them I needed to say goodbye to the rabbit—it was the only one who understood, after all—but they wouldn't let me, and my mother took my hand and led me away.

I guess I could have said I changed my mind and that I wanted to stay, but I couldn't go on taking things and not get caught, and if I didn't go with them they would die on Eagles' Nest Road, the treacherous cliffside road on the way to camp. Huh? A new thing in my head? So I reluctantly got into the car, and the camp and the kids and the pine woods disappeared at the first turn in the road.

The next morning I woke up in my narrow bedroom above the store, the only outdoor space the tar roof outside my window. I lay there and thought about the green outfield and Bruce Cohen's chest.

Brooklyn was the last place anybody would want to be that July. Brooklyn had its own special kind of hot. That summer was so hot you could fry an egg on the sidewalk in front of the store. There wasn't a cloud in the sky and the sun was yellow and relentless. It was in the newspapers that six people keeled over from heat exposure at Ebbets Field, and the elevated line was packed with people carrying bedsheets, towels, and a cold thermos, taking the half-hour ride to Coney Island to cool off.

My father resented me for making him lose the $800 fee for Camp Lokanda, and for punishment he didn't speak to me for the rest of that summer. The way I felt about it was, he didn't deserve any other son than this one.

Two

Joyce Brothers

By the time I was eleven years old I was swimming in twos and drowning in twenties. The numbers tumbled through my head as in a cartoon, solid, sentient, shapes that tasted like metal. Twos, two, two twos. Twenty was the best. Counting to twenty was magic and calming; it would keep me and my mother safe. It was the prime number in our lives, because my mother and I were both born on the twentieth day of the month, and exactly ten years to the day before I was born, on November 20, 1936, my twelve-year-old mother dropped her scarf during her solo as Little Buttercup in *HMS Pinafore* at Montauk Junior High School, and my dad, who was then fifteen, stepped out of the chorus of sailors and picked it up for her. Years later, when they married and looked at the date on the *HMS Pinafore* program that my mother had saved, they discovered that their names were directly across from each other in the columns that listed the players: Isidore Goldberg (sailor) and Ruth Goshin (Miss Buttercup). Him, her, me, it was meant to be. We were *bashert*.

Also, two was part of twenty, the soul of twenty, if you

think about it. That's why I touched twice. Touch once, touch twice, unless it was a doorknob; the second time you touched the doorknob, you could turn it, but if you couldn't turn it with the second touch you had to start over by wiping your hand with a tissue. Who made up these crazy rules? They were tyranny.

All this counting and touching took up a lot of time, so when you hear about people with obsessive behavior and it seems colorfully eccentric, like Jack Nicholson in *As Good As It Gets*, in which he's a writer with OCD who has to hopscotch down the street so as not to step on a crack, the part that nobody mentions is that it can take ten minutes just to get out the front door. I developed Kabuki-like movements to try to hide the rituals from people—like brushing my hand up against something nonchalantly instead of actually touching it twice. When I counted numbers I counted silently, without moving my lips, so people wouldn't know, but everyone could see something was going on in my mind, and that part of me was somewhere else.

Since there was no one around who could tell me what was wrong, I decided to ask Dr. Joyce Brothers, who wrote a popular syndicated advice column that appeared in the *Daily News*. I hand-printed a letter outlining my dilemma, asking her what was wrong with me and how to fix it, and I mailed it to the newspaper. When I didn't read an answer over the next few days, I impatiently called the *Daily News* and persevered long enough to get through to Dr. Brothers's secretary. She said that Dr. Brothers had received my letter but they weren't going to publish it, and I should contact my family doctor for help.

I used this piece of information as though it had come

from an expert, and insisted my parents make an appointment for me to see Dr. Kaufman, our milquetoast general practitioner on Ocean Parkway. He had salt-and-pepper–colored hair and my mother had a secret crush on him. My mother and father and I waited hours in his packed waiting room, reading through stacks of the *Saturday Evening Post*, before he took us into his hushed office with bookcases and green drapes. Instead of allowing me to talk, my father told him his version of what was happening. My dad said he was under enormous stress because of my behavior. He dreaded coming home from work. My mother started to dab at her tears. Dr. Kaufman nodded as my father described my compulsions—"He touches things" and "He clears his throat strangely."

When my father was finished the doctor looked at me and asked, "Why do you do all these strange things?"

Good question. I didn't know why I did all those strange things. I certainly wasn't going to try to explain my feelings about lonely ice cream pop sticks to him. Yet I did want to impart how hopeless and sad I felt, and that the prickly feeling in my chest often made it hard to breathe. Was there anything he could do for that? But I didn't say any of that. All I could muster was, "I don't feel well."

Dr. Kaufman had no diagnosis. But the local diagnosis on 18th Avenue was that I was crazy. No fancier diagnosis needed than that. Crazy. Sick in the head. A "nut job," my father's sister called me one day. Everybody in the store knew it, everybody on the block knew it, and everybody knew it at junior high school, where I was able to attend for only a few weeks before I began to seize up, like an engine with no oil, and I stopped going to school completely. I went on home instruction, and a nice woman from the Board of Education came to the apartment above the store twice a week and taught me math and made me read Thornton Wilder's *Our Town*. She politely pretended she didn't see me touch things. Twice.

Being in a ladies' clothing store most of my day, I had to be resourceful for amusement, and the cardboard shipping boxes that merchandise arrived in became my métier. I discovered I liked spending time inside corrugated boxes, with the top closed, a sort of a child's tree house, retail-store style. New corrugated boxes packed with merchandise arrived at the store every day, all shapes and sizes. Sometimes the box would be right out in the open, sometimes hidden behind a rack of dresses, where I could do my reconnaissance undisturbed. I spent a couple of years in and out of boxes, listening, watching, thinking, reading my grandmother's hand-me-down books with a flashlight. I read the entire oeuvre of Harold Robbins and Superboy comics in a box. I time-traveled in boxes. Sometimes I transformed them into jukeboxes, hiding a small record player inside with an extension cord to the wall outlet. The customers were encouraged to drop a nickel into a slot I cut on the side of the box, and I would play a 45 rpm of "Tennessee Waltz," the only record I had.

On other days in the box I'd make a tiny iris with a straight pin and sit quietly for hours, eavesdropping and observing the melodramas of the busy store. Unseen in my many boxes I listened to petty jealousies between the salesgirls—who made what sale, who was allowed to make change, who last went for an English at the Culver. I listened to them talk about their husbands and children, and gossip jealously about my grandparents, rich merchants who had no money trouble. I listened to women confide their most intimate marital problems to my grandmother, who dispensed homespun wisdom and sometimes a harmless off-color joke. I got to know all the punch lines. "Don't stop, I'll write you a check" or "Lady, I'm an old man, how about a cup of tea better?"

I heard them talk about me. Not just the "come to no good" stuff, but how I was crazy, and that it was my parents' fault for not getting me under control, and what I needed was a good spanking, but Rose and Harry spoiled me, and that my father was nuts too, what could you expect?

I compiled the prosaic neighborhood gossip in my head as if it meant something. I knew that Lily Williams's husband, Earl, who was a limousine driver, got a $100 Christmas gift from the man who was president of Whirlpool. I knew that Dodie Berkowitz wouldn't let her daughter Ida get laughing gas at the dentist because she thought it made her stupid, and that her husband, Benny, a trainman on the New York-to-Baltimore U.S. mail run, once had a heart attack while they were having sex, and she had to bang on the wall behind the bed to summon a neighbor to help pull him off of her. I worried that Koret of California would not ship to us anymore because we were ninety days behind in paying their invoices. I knew the bra cup sizes we carried stopped at triple D, except on special order, and I knew that Smokey taupe/seamless/no heel pantyhose were on the top shelf. I knew that the glove salesman was the father of the actor Arnold Stang, and that the Jantzen bathing suit salesman wrote the lyrics to "Love Letters in the Sand," but he didn't make much money because he accepted a flat fee.

I witnessed the clucking and preening of the hens when my grandfather was present, the only man in a world of perfumed women. I was confused by the curious world of women's plumbing problems. Such secrets. Hysterectomies. Hot flashes. The changes. "She was dry down there." Her time of the month. A period. A period is an end to a sentence, I thought, now it was an end to what? Then one day I was in a box watching through the fuzzy peephole I made with a needle when I got a demonstration. The assistant principal of the local grade school stopped into the store to buy stockings. A very proper and nice lady, she was standing near the cash register paying for her purchase and chatting, when I heard a *plit plit plit plit* sound. I could see drops of blood falling from between her legs under her skirt, dripping on the marble-patterned Kentile squares that covered the floor.

The assistant principal murmured "Oh no," and there was a terrible silence as Lily Williams helped her to the toilet in the back. When the humiliated woman emerged a few minutes later she kneeled and wiped up the trail of blood spots on the floor with toilet paper. The other women tried to console her, saying accidents happen, but I could see she was mortified beyond consolation. When she finished cleaning up as best she could, she apologized again and hurried out the door. I was bewildered, but when I climbed out of the box and asked the salesgirls what just happened, they yelled that I was hiding and spying on them, and I sulked with the lid closed the rest of the afternoon.

The Goldberg Variations

In a zany complication, when I was about twelve years old and couldn't figure out who I was, my father changed our name from Goldberg to Gaines. He did it in part to spite his family—they were always feuding, those Goldbergs—and in part because he was swept away by the wave of assimilation of first-generation, American-born Jews anxious to disguise their Eastern European roots. The Holocaust may have blunted open anti-Semitism in America, but it hardly eliminated it, even in New York. The legendary Jewish banker Otto Kahn nailed it: "A kike is a Jewish gentleman who has just left the room." After World War II the Jews were either defiantly proud of their heritage, or they wanted to disguise it. My grandfather Gog had long ago changed his last name, from Goshinsky to Goshin. Of course, for the Orthodox and hard core, changing your name was traitorous.

The name Goldberg carried an unusual burden at the time because of the huge success of the 1950s TV series called *The Goldbergs*, a sitcom that took place in the Bronx and would indelibly stereotype New York Jews, just as *Amos and Andy* had branded blacks ten years before. Molly Goldberg, played by the actress Gertrude Berg, was a wise and loving mother, but she was also an immigrant with a singsong Jewish intonation who gossiped with the neighbors in her apartment building out of her window. The show's trademark opening was a woman's voice yodeling, "Yoo-hoo, Mrs. Goldberg!" It became irritating when, for the thousandth time, someone greeted us, "Yoo-hoo, Mrs. Goldberg!"

My dad talked about changing our name for years, but what finally pushed him over was an incident at a laundry in Lake George, New York. We were on one of my dad's aimless driving vacations, which we took every year at the end of August, coming from Franconia Notch, New Hampshire. On the long drive to Lake George my father filled me with dread, saying how anti-Semitic Lake George was and that we shouldn't let anybody know that we were Jewish. "We shouldn't even be going there," he said, "except that I wouldn't let them stop us from going there just because we're Jewish."

I was even more alarmed when we checked into a lakeside cabin and he told the woman at the desk that our name was "Green." We slept that night with a chair propped up against the doorknob of the cabin, I guess in case of a pogrom.

The next day, when we dropped off our dirty laundry at a local laundromat, my father again gave the name Green. When we returned to pick up the clean laundry the following day, they handed it back to us unwashed, with an excuse about the washing machines being broken, although we could see clearly otherwise. My father was outraged. What had transpired, he divined when we got back to the car, was that the laundry owners were anti-Semites, and they could see in our faces that we were Jews, and they refused to do our Jewish laundry.

Never would our dirty clothes be turned down again! he declared. We would change our name. We would still be Jewish, but not Jewish. The idea thrilled me. A clean start. A reinvention. Maybe with a less Jewish name my dad would be named assistant principal. On the ride home we spent hours nominating new surnames. The rule was that it had to start with a "G," like Goldberg, although it wasn't as if we had monogrammed towels we didn't want to throw away. The name Green sounded too Jewish, we decided, as though it was shortened from Greenstein; and that's why we didn't want Gold, which sounded shortened from Goldberg. "Graham," my mother's choice, was too grand, and "Granit," my favorite, sounded hard and made-up. At the end of a six-hour ride home, having run out of G names, we turned down Flatbush Avenue and drove past a car and tire dealership named Gaines Oldsmobile. We all liked that name, and we were tired. That's where I got my name from, an Oldsmobile dealership.

My father hired a lawyer, and a year or two later I became Steven Seith Gaines and received a new birth certificate with that name. My mother claimed my middle name was from a spelling in the Old Testament, but it doesn't exist. I liked the sound of the word Seith, and because I wanted to be as far away from Steven Goldberg as I could get, I decided that I would be called Seith instead of Steven. For a few years I was known as Seith Gaines. My mother became Ruth Gaines, and my father went from Isidore Hyman Goldberg to I. Hal Gaines.

Suddenly, people who knew us yesterday as Goldberg were expected to call us Gaines, me Seith, and my dad Hal. What made it even stranger was that my father made us pretend we were always named Gaines. How he expected this to succeed I don't know. Even my mother had problems remembering to call my dad Hal, instead of Izzy. The name stuck in her throat every time she tried to say it. He had a habit of walking in front of her in the street, forgetting where she was, and she would call after him, "Iz . . . er . . . Hal!" He often didn't turn around, forgetting what his new name was himself.

My father was very sensitive about people mocking him for changing his name and he considered it an insult if anybody referred to him as Izzy Goldberg. He forbade my mother to go to the local grocer, who taunted him by calling him "Goldberg." And of course his family never let him live it down. If they ran into him in the dry cleaners or passed him in the street, they'd scream, "Goldberg! Goldberg!" at him.

As for Seith Gaines, after the initial thrill wore off, it was hugely disappointing. I dropped the Seith and went back to Steven, and I was quite disappointed when it turned out that Steven Gaines wasn't any different from Steven Goldberg at all.

The King's English

If things weren't already wacky enough, sitting in a box one day when I was thirteen years old, I decided that I wanted to be a child actor because I was jealous of the Mouseketeers on Disney's *Mickey Mouse Club* show, which I watched on TV every afternoon. Also, I had a crush on Brandon deWilde, the blond child actor from Long Island who was only eleven years old when he was nominated for an Oscar for his supporting role in *Shane*, a movie I saw with my mother at the Culver Theater on a Friday night. When I told my parents about my aspirations to stage and screen, instead of rolling their eyes, they were excited that I had taken an interest in something outside of Rose's Bras Girdles Sportswear, although my father was less keen than my mother was about my far-fetched new pursuit. However, to encourage any enthusiasm outside of my corrugated world, my mother suggested that I go for acting lessons on the Lower East Side of Manhattan, at the Henry Street Settlement House, which offered a variety of community services. On Saturdays there was an acting class for kids that cost only a few bucks.

I was enrolled the following week, and after two classes the acting teacher, a young girl in black tights with some tenuous connection to the theater, told my parents that although I had tremendous acting potential my Brooklyn accent would hold me back from having a professional career. I was in urgent need of speech and phonetics classes, more than acting.

So it was that every Saturday morning my dad sullenly drove me to the Henry Street Settlement and parked outside, smoking cigarettes and reading the *Mirror* while I spent hours repeating the phrase *"Pul-eeze ahl-low fahr Ahhn to poss,"* until my "e"s were rounded, and my "a"s softened. Eventually I sounded like Basil Rathbone. Having a faux English accent didn't sit well with anyone on 18th Avenue. It embarrassed by father, made the salesgirls cluck their tongues, and when I came into the deli for a hot dog with sauerkraut, Mr. Silverstein would hoot "Cheerio!" at me. But I vowed not to revert to Brooklynese and hurt my career.

During this period while I was studying to be a child actor my mother got a phone call from the guidance counselor at Montauk Junior High School. Even though I was intermittently on home instruction, there was an opportunity that might interest me. New York State had embarked on a massive experiment and installed televisions in every school in the city. They had leased the facilities of New York's WPIX-TV, Channel 11, and were broadcasting educational shows from 9 to 3 daily in the tristate area. An educator named Jack Arenstein was going to be the teacher on a twice-weekly show called *The King's English*, for junior high school students, and there was a citywide search for a student to be on the show with him. Would I be interested in auditioning?

Overnight my rituals and counting became only background noise as I shifted from inside the box into a media personality. Haircut, shoes, sports jacket, and tie. Memorize "The Cremation of Sam McGee" by Robert W. Service, in case I'm asked to perform. By the time I got to my audition a few days later I was full of spunk and desire. I was, indeed, asked to perform for Jack Arenstein and the producers. I gave an inspired and wry performance of Service's poem in which a gold prospector cremates a friend to discover that a furnace is the only place in Alaska his pal can stay warm. I knew an adjective from an adverb too, which didn't hurt, nor did my ersatz English accent. When I was told that I had been chosen to be the student in *The King's English*, I spent a good long time on the living room floor, squealing with joy like a piglet, hugging myself, laughing hysterically and then crying, then hugging myself in the bathroom mirror. It was a miracle, unbelievable this was actually happening to me. From Rose's Bras Girdles Sportswear to stardom. From the smell of sizing to the perfume of greasepaint. I would be the Brandon deWilde of educational TV.

Early in the morning on Tuesdays and Thursdays my mother and I took the subway to New York City and walked along 42nd Street past the Chrysler Building to the *New York Daily News* building, where the WPIX studios were located. The director and crew were all jovial and high energy and the stage manager gave me some pointers about where to look, and warned me never to look directly at the camera. I sat in a chair in the makeup room while a schoolmarmish makeup woman put pancake makeup on my nose and combed my hair with a long part down the right side of my head, like an *Archie* comic book character. I learned the rule that we could wear any color except white, because of the TV cameras for some reason. The lights in the studio were brilliant and hot, and just before we went on the air people were tense, but I fed on the nervous energy.

When the red light under the big bulky camera that was aimed at me lit up for the first time it was electrifying. Tens of thousands of people were watching me. I was either going to disassemble, or seize the moment and become the star I was meant to be. And a star I became, to everyone's amazement, including my own. Over the next several weeks I played Jim Hawkins in a dramatization of Robert Louis Stevenson's *Treasure Island* with a passion unseen before on broadcast television, wearing a ruffled blouse from my grandmother's store. I was composed and confident, I remembered my dialogue, and acting came to me naturally. Maybe it was the hundreds of movies I had seen. Another memorable segment involved me in a roller coaster in Coney Island, in which Mr. Arenstein and I taught the students how to tell an anecdote while I ate cotton candy.

Without any doubt I was insufferable. Just to watch me order a bialy and chocolate milk in my English accent was enough to make any observer want to strangle me. I expected to bask in the adulation of my peers. Instead, I was taunted and mocked by eighth- and ninth-graders from all five boroughs who were forced to watch me twice a week. Since the show aired on live TV everywhere in the New York metropolitan area, even adults began to know who I was, and I became a target. The resentment was so potent that I was sucker-punched in the mouth at a Saturday matinee at the Culver Theater, and one day two tough girls

took my Philco transistor radio from me and threw it down
a sewer.

But now that I was a TV star I was better able to manage and hide my rituals. Vanity and sheer adrenaline at first
tamped down my obsessive behavior, but one day on the
set of *The King's English* I needed to touch a piece of chalk
twice, and everybody noticed it. The next week I tried to
take a pancake makeup sponge from the dressing room, and
I was caught by the makeup lady, who made a fuss about it,
as though I had stolen her wallet. She was the teaspoon of
tar in the barrel of honey, the Lily Williams of the television
station. With her watching over my shoulder, the compulsions started to punch through, and in only a few days of
increasingly odd behavior it became clear that I had issues
too debilitating for me to continue on the show.

Mr. Arenstein called me at home and apologized. I
sobbed and begged him to give me a second chance, but
he said he was sorry. I learned later they had already found
another boy for the show. My fragile, newfound self-worth
was demolished in a single blow. It was soul crushing. I
couldn't show my face after that. I even stopped going to
the Culver Theater. I retreated to a corrugated box behind
the rack of dresses, where I sat in the dark counting and
touching, furious with myself, thinking about suicide seriously for the first time.

Tina

In the late afternoons, when Tina's kitchen filled with
shadows and a pot of thick meat sauce simmered on the

stove, we sat at the kitchen table and talked while she did the rebus puzzle. Tina had multiple sclerosis, and she was going downhill fast. Only one year after she had been diagnosed, she walked like a spinning top about to totter over, and she had to hold on to furniture to make her way across the room. I went to her apartment almost every day around 3 p.m. and helped her straighten up and cook dinner. The multiple sclerosis made her left eye sag, and the medication dried her mouth, so she licked her lips all the time. She was my mother's age, but when we chatted it wasn't like talking to a mother, it was like having a friend. She thought I was funny and laughed at things I said. She asked me about my fears and why I counted and touched things, and I was able to explain it to her better than anybody else. She made no judgment.

Tina told me about her own fears, about how afraid she was of dying of MS, but that she had faith in Jesus. Sometimes she felt steadier on her feet, and the doctor said there was a possibility of a remission and her MS might get better for a while, maybe forever, so she still had hope. She wished she were well enough to go to the church on 15th Avenue and light candles. She said there were statues of saints there that could help her, and that her patron saint was St. Jude, the saint of hopeless causes. I decided he would be my patron saint too.

Tina and her husband, "Big Rich" Mastriano, were my parents' best friends. They saw each other every Saturday night, usually at the Mastrianos' apartment on Foster Avenue, where they sat around the kitchen table smoking cigarettes and drinking coffee. Big Rich was a hairy-chested *mook* who worked as a mechanic replacing springs on trucks. He used Lava soap to remove the grease from his fingernails and knuckles when he came home from the garage on Coney Island Avenue.

Tina confided in me about Big Rich and their son Little Rich, how terribly they treated her, and how angry they were with her for being sick. Big Rich complained a lot to my dad about Tina. He told my dad that he was a young man himself, and although it was a shame Tina got sick, he didn't want it to ruin his life too. Tina told me one afternoon that she was worried Big Rich was cheating on her with the bookkeeper from the garage, who was a *puttana*. My dad said the garage was "mobbed up" and he wouldn't put anything past them.

Tina worried that Little Rich was going to end up in jail. He skipped school and stole from stores. He was a strapping fourteen-year-old guido, slow and suspicious, with dirty fingernails and a sneer. He considered me, if at all, with contempt, as his mother's handmaiden. Unfortunately I was wildly sexually attracted to his adolescent beefiness and thick neck.

The Mastrianos lived on the second floor of a wood frame house, above Mr. Galluccio, an Italian widower in his seventies with a white handlebar mustache. He made his own wine in the basement, and in the autumn the whole house was filled with the pungent sour smell of grapes fermenting. But Tina didn't notice, she said. The multiple sclerosis had robbed her of her smell. Out back there was a stable where Mr. Galluccio kept an old beleaguered donkey that he dressed in a felt hat and fake flowers, with the donkey's ears sticking through. He made the donkey pull a cart up and down the block to give the children free rides. One day I was watching out the window when the donkey's penis came out, slick and pink, like a misshapen bologna, and I gasped at its size and ugliness. Tina laughed and made fun of me all afternoon.

Tina usually needed to lie down before Big Rich and Little Rich came home, and while she napped I went up to the attic and shot pool. There was a regulation-size pool table under the eaves. It was Big Rich's pride and joy. It had a pristine emerald-green felt top with ivory inlays of cue balls in the bumper wood. For a year or two I spent almost every afternoon up there shooting pool while Tina napped, softly singing songs to myself and watching the sky get dark through a little window at the far end of the attic. Eventually I became a pretty good pool shooter, and some nights when Big Rich got home I could even beat him, which annoyed the hell out of him. A lot of things about me annoyed Big Rich.

One Saturday night I bragged to Little Rich about the stash of pornography my father kept in a crinkled brown paper bag in the back right side of the top drawer of his dresser. While the adults were sitting around the kitchen talking, Little Rich and I snuck over to my parents' apartment to look at it. We lay down next to each other on the bed and went through the contents of the paper bag, leaning in close to examine each piece, so close I could smell the Fritos on his breath. In my father's stash there were a few black-and-white photographs with tiny holes at the top, as though they had been thumbtacked to a wall. One was a picture of a naked couple standing up with their faces turned away from the camera, the man hugging the woman from behind. Also in the frame of the picture was the bathrobe and belly of a man standing to the side. In another photo a woman lying on her back on a rock had an enormous shrub of pubic hair, but I could see no entrance. There was a photograph of the actor Robert Mitchum hugging a woman, with her bare breasts pressed against his shirtless chest.

What held my attention most were the hand-drawn, pocket-sized comic booklets printed on colored construction paper, the pages held together with a rusty staple. One booklet featured Donald Duck, who had a surreal man's hard-on extending from his belly feathers, which he used to fuck Daisy Duck. And in the Popeye booklet, before he fucked Olive Oyl he ate a can of spinach that made his cock get bigger and harder. It only seemed natural that I should suggest to Little Rich that he and I take our penises out. I was breathless with anticipation while he unbuttoned his pants and pulled down his underwear from which a throbbing penis sprang up and slapped against his stomach almost up to his navel, pulsing upwards a few times like it was yanked on a string. It was the first erect penis of another person around my age that I had ever seen, and it was huge.

Big Rich knew a lot of crooked cops through the garage on Coney Island Avenue. One sweaty August midnight Big Rich and Little Rich and my father and I drove to Prospect Park, where we met up with two cops waiting for us in a black-and-white squad car. The park was deserted at that hour, and we followed the squad car off the road up onto the grass of Long Meadow, a scruffy green field that was the biggest open expanse in the park. "A million of 'em," one of the cops said, nodding toward the dark meadow. I squinted in the gloom and realized that the meadow was alive with foraging rabbits.

The other cop popped open the trunk of the squad car and took out a rifle. He checked the ammo, cocked and uncocked it, and handed it to Big Rich. The first cop used the squad car's spotlight to roam through the field of rabbits and pick one out for a kill. A ball of white fur froze in the intense beam, its eyes two red reflector buttons. Big Rich aimed through the gunsight, the rifle bucked in his arms, and a sound like a cracking whip echoed through Prospect Park.

The rabbit in the spotlight jumped straight up in the air when the bullet hit. Then it lay twitching on the ground until it died. The men all said what a good shot Big Rich was, and he handed the rifle to my father. The cop picked out another rabbit with the spotlight, my dad took aim, squeezed the trigger, and missed. You could see where the bullet hit the ground short of the rabbit and blew a puff of dirt into the air. Red-faced and mumbling excuses, my father handed the rifle to me.

The spotlight picked out another bunny sitting motionless, its nose twitching. Everybody was saying, "Hurry! Hurry!" but all I could think about was the rabbit from Camp Lokanda who was my friend, so I aimed two feet over its head and pulled the trigger. But the trigger wouldn't pull—my father hadn't re-cocked the hammer before handing it to me—and Little Rich yanked the rifle out of my hands, re-cocked it, aimed haphazardly, and shot the rabbit. With its last breath it tried to hop away before it keeled over. "Ha!" Little Rich laughed smugly. I waited at the car while Big and Little Rich shot another half dozen rabbits. On the way home I stared out the window. Big Rich asked me over his shoulder from the front seat, "What's with you?" I didn't answer.

One afternoon not long after the bunny-shooting expedition, Tina put a big pot of water up to boil to cook pasta, and when she tried to take it off the stove she lost her balance and the boiling water poured on her chest and stomach and legs, scalding her to the bone. When I got there for my regular afternoon visit she was unconscious on the kitchen floor, barely alive. I called my mother at the store, and while she called Big Rich at work, I called the fire department down the block, and soon an ambulance arrived. Tina was taken to the burn unit at Kings County. Big Rich said to me, "And where were *you*?" as if I should have been there.

I never saw Tina again. In the time it took to recover from the burns her MS got so much worse she needed full-time care and was moved to a nursing home. Big Rich divorced her and married his girlfriend and moved to Florida. Little Rich stayed in Brooklyn and got married and had four kids, and when he was in his late thirties he had a heart attack and died. I don't know how Tina eventually found peace. I lost track of her, but she lives brightly in my memory.

After Tina scalded herself I had nowhere to go in the afternoons, so I began to ride the 18th Avenue bus. I would get on at the corner and take a window seat and stare out the window, looking. I never got off the bus. I waited until the end of the line all the way on the other side of Brooklyn, where the bus turned around and took me back. I observed as familiar places morphed into somewhere else. I stared curiously at houses and people in strange neighborhoods, flashes of apartments through open curtains and venetian blinds flew by, beds, table, lampshade, woman in a bathrobe. I wondered who I

would be if I lived there, that window, that house, that
life instead of mine. I searched up and down the streets
we passed, hoping for a glimpse of the lawnmower boy,
thinking that maybe I would find the courage to get off
the bus and speak to him.

Three

Knish Man

Cushioned in cotton and pressed behind glass, like a butterfly in the nature shack. My mother and father, the pale ochre of a daguerreotype, the Jewish American Gothic, standing in my hospital room, drawn into themselves with shame. Voices fading in and out like boggy radio signals. Sometimes my grandfather hovered near me, or sat in a chair, reading the torah, or maybe it was just a newspaper. I couldn't tell from my morphine funhouse.

I pretended not to hear the people who wafted by my bed asking why. Instead, I played the automatic-door game at the store, the one where if I looked into the thick edge of the glass the customers and saleswomen splintered into rainbow slices, while I hid under the glove counter and pulled the door open with a rope. I stuck my head inside my grandmother's suitcase and tasted the coconut sweetness of Miami Beach at night. There were colored lanterns in Miami Beach, and pink man-of-wars like half-blown bubbles from Bazooka gum strewn up and down the beach, and Royal Palms two stories high. The egg-salad sandwich was gritty, from eggshell or from sand, I couldn't tell which, except now it was a blistering August Sunday in Coney Island, not Miami, and I was beet red from the sun, slathered in Noxzema. I sat under an umbrella on a chenille spread held down at the corners with our shoes. The knish man, leathery and stoop-shouldered, weighted down by double shopping bags of oily knishes and soda on dry ice, trudged through sand as hot as coals. "Hot kin-ishes! Hot kin-ishes!" he cried out. "Hot kin-ishes! Cold drinks!"

The knish man was standing next to my bed in the hospital wearing a white lab coat, dolefully staring at me. He wanted to know if I would help him carry his shopping bags when he got old, because the bags were getting too heavy. When he died I could have his job. But I didn't want to stumble back and forth in the sand at Coney Island, and I shook my head, but my father said yes, when I grew up, I would be the knish man's apprentice. The knish man stared at the bandages on my arms. I had been sewn up like Frankenstein's monster, with zigzagging black threads.

"*Vus makst du?*" he asked me, staring at the stitches. He was wearing a round black hat with a flat brim, like a Dr. Seuss character, and he had a long beard with a crumb caught in it.

"Tell the rabbi why you did this," my father said.

The knish man said that phumphy if I didn't tell him phumphy phumphy I couldn't be his assistant, and I was glad. He had only contempt for me. For him I would have been better off dead. Suicide was an abomination to Orthodox Jews; to try to destroy yourself was considered not just crazy but irretrievably unholy. They always hated me at Hebrew school, where like a wolf pack they smelled out my homosexuality and expelled me as a weak pup. Without a rabbi to teach me, I had to mimic a scratchy old recording to be able to say my *haftorah* in synagogue and be finished with the farce of becoming a man. The knish man tied black leather boxes around my father's head as a sign between his eyes and wrapped his left arm down to his fingers. They chanted in the language of my exclusion, and my father wept. He pressed a twenty-dollar bill into the hand of the knish man, who dispersed like smoke in a breeze.

"What do I say at school?" my aggrieved father asked my mother after the rabbi left. He was a guidance counselor in a Brooklyn high school, and his fifteen-year-old kid tried to kill himself. How do you explain that? His cheeks puffed up as he blew air out of his lips in a silent whistle of grief.

My bewildered mom, *gutte neshuma* that she was, in over her head for many years by that point, sat in a chair across the room looking exhausted, her eyes puffy from crying, wiping her tears with a crumpled tissue. Her jet-black hair was pulled back behind her head in a chignon, and her eyebrows were drawn in an exaggerated arc, which gave her a vaguely Oriental look.

My dad pulled his chair to the edge of the bed and tried to put his hand on top of mine but he couldn't really relax his palm, so it just rested there. Even when he petted a dog he did it with a rigid palm. He sat next to me, slack-jawed, dwelling on the consequences of my actions for a long while. "Is this my fault?" he asked my mom.

"I don't know what to say," she answered. "We have a sick child."

I fell into a deep sleep and when I woke in the middle of the night my parents were gone, the room was dark, and the halls were quiet. An orderly appeared at the door carry ing towels and fresh sheets. "Hi," he said from the shadows.

"Hi," I answered dreamily.

He stopped a distance from the bed. "I heard you were here," he said. "I saw your mother and father leave the building tonight."

My mother and father? "Who are you?" I asked.

"It's Michael, who lives downstairs from Gertie."

My god, it was Michael/Michelle.

"What are you doing here?" I asked.

"I work here," he said. "In the laundry room." I remembered now—he worked in a hospital. What was he doing coming into my room? "I thought maybe you could use some company," he said. "I thought maybe you could use somebody to talk to."

I knew what he meant, that I needed somebody of my own kind to share my secret. "I don't need *you* to talk to!" I said. "Why should I talk to *you*?"

"Everybody needs somebody to talk to," he said. "I do."

"Well I don't!"

"I only came to bring clean towels and pillowcases," he said primly, putting them on a shelf in the closet. "I was just leaving." He walked out of the room without looking at me. I've thought about that moment many times, and how I would like to thank him for trying, but I never saw him again.

Dr. Doris

Dr. Doris Milman was a paraplegic in a wheelchair. My mother said she was paralyzed giving birth. I didn't understand how giving birth could paralyze a woman, so I chalked it up to the treachery of female plumbing I heard so much about in the store. Dr. Doris's wheelchair was a clunky thing with huge rubber wheels and squeaky gears. The way her paralyzed legs were positioned to the side, the stiff way she sat in the chair, gave her a sort of ominous, Dr. Strangelove quality. Doris Milman was a star in the field of adolescent psychiatry and an expert in adolescent suicide. She had been brought in from Kings County Hospital to consult on my case. I was impressed they were calling in a specialist but still too goofy on morphine to get enthusiastic about much of anything.

When she first arrived in my hospital room, a file folder jammed into the seat next to her, my father ham-handedly offered to push her wheelchair next to my bed, to which she responded firmly, "No thank you, I can manage it." And she did, with considerable determination and strength for a small woman, deftly maneuver herself next to my bed and locked the chair in place. She was wearing a navy blue suit a white blouse, and cutesy ID tag, "Dr. Doris," pinned to her lapel. I wondered who dressed her, or how she went to the bathroom.

"My name is Doctor Doris. Are you Steven?" she asked.

I nodded. Her brief, tight smile told me that compassion aside, she was pure business. "How are you doing?" she asked, opening my file. "Are you in much pain?"

"Some," I said.

"I've read your file and you've been through an awful lot. I'm sorry," she said. "I'm here today to help you begin to feel better."

"Okay," I said.

She scanned my file for a moment and asked, "When was the last time you went to school?"

"On and off, for a couple of years," I said.

"And what about counting and touching things?"

"That stopped," I lied. "But not altogether," I amended. "Sometimes, when I feel nervous."

"And what about saving things, do you still do that?"

"Not anymore," I said.

"I see." She tucked the file back into the seat next to her. "You must have been very angry to hurt yourself like that," she said, nodding toward my arms.

I shrugged noncommittally.

"I want to help you feel better about yourself," she said. "But in order to do that, I need to know what made you so unhappy that you wanted to hurt yourself so badly."

I shrugged again and focused on the sink across the room.

"I know that you don't want to talk about it, but can you understand why we need to know what made you hurt yourself?" she asked.

I nodded.

"Will you tell me, then?" she said. "You can whisper it to me, if you want. Or I can ask your parents to leave the room."

That's when things started to go awry.

I pretended I was deaf and mouthed the words, "*I'm sor-rey, I cahn't hear yew.*" I said it partly because I had been asked so many times why I tried to kill myself without responding that I was deaf to the question, and partly because it was a punch line to one of my grandmother's enduring stories. She was watching TV in her house in Freeport and she could see from her chair that a Seventh Day

Adventist rang the front doorbell. Gog said to her, "Don't answer the door, they'll talk your ear off for an hour!" But my grandmother went and she was back in a minute. She told Gog, "I pretended I was deaf, and I said, '*I'm sor-rey, I cahn't hear yew.*'" And the Seventh Day Adventist nodded and smiled and left. My grandmother told that story a dozen times and always got a big laugh.

So when Dr. Doris was about the hundredth person to ask me why I tried to kill myself, I said, "*I'm sor-rey, I cahn't hear yew,*" like I was deaf. It did not get a laugh.

"I think you can hear me perfectly well," Dr. Doris said, not happy.

"It's a family joke," my mother explained anxiously.

Dr. Doris unlocked and did a 180-degree turn to get a good look at my parents. My mother, in size 16 Joshua Tree coordinates, had come directly from work at the store and she still had a pencil stuck in her chignon, like a Chinese hair stick. "Can you people shed some light on what's going on at home?" Dr. Doris asked.

My father's cheek quivered with a tiny spasm of anger. I knew it was the way Dr. Doris had said, "*you people.*" I'd seen him bristle like that before.

"I'm a child guidance counselor in a city high school," he said, presenting his credentials. "I work with children every day. I can tell you that this was out of the clear blue. Nothing was going on at home."

Hmm, I thought, I bet he really believes that. I glanced at my mother, who remained silent.

"Nothing?" Dr. Doris scoffed. "Compulsions and hoarding aren't nothing. And there are always warning signs leading up to a suicide bid. Do you have any idea why your son would try to take his own life? What comes to mind?"

"We've asked him," my father said. "Everybody has asked him. But he won't say." He turned to me. "Son, please tell us why you did this so we can help."

I felt sorry for him at that moment; he was being so earnest, calling me "son" when he never called me that. So I thought I would help him out. I tried to think of some explanation for what I did, other than the truth, and as I lay there in the hospital bed, my arms sewn up with black stitches like the Frankenstein monster, a very bad idea came into my head—that I should answer, "I did it because I'm the Frankenstein monster." But saying that, after pretending I was deaf, would only incense my father and make Dr. Doris think I was really nuts. Or was I really nuts? So I said, "I did it because I'm the Frankenstein monster."

"I'll give you Frankenstein monster, mister," my father said.

"Now, now," Dr. Doris hushed him. She stared at me for a moment and nodded, like she had made a resolute decision. "I'd like you to consider getting your son long-term care," she told my father. "There's a likelihood of another attempt, and it's not responsible to just soldier on and hope it doesn't happen again. He should be someplace safe until we can figure out what's wrong."

"What does that mean?" my father asked.

"A hospital," she said.

"A *mental* hospital?" he asked.

"I wouldn't characterize it that way, no," Dr. Doris answered. She turned to me and said, "There's a very nice place called Hillside. I think you might benefit greatly from it. Perhaps it might be good for you to be away from home for a while, so you can collect your thoughts, and give you time to think about what's troubling you, and have somebody to talk it over with."

"You've got to be joking," my father said. "We're not putting him in a mental hospital."

"You need to consider what's best for your child's safety," she said.

"You don't even *know* my child. You've been here five minutes and you're telling me you want to put my child in a mental hospital."

"There are legal ramifications to attempted suicide by a minor," Dr. Doris said. "If it's in the boy's best interests, if he's in substantial danger—and I think he's exhibited that he is—the state could be petitioned that he be committed. And nobody wants that to happen."

"My son will never be in a mental hospital," my father said.

"We should talk again tomorrow," Dr. Doris suggested. "Perhaps you need to sleep on it."

"I don't need to sleep on it," my father assured her.

"Okay, then," Dr. Doris said, beginning to execute a three-point turn to leave the room.

Now here came the *really* strange part. Since I was already different, if I was going to end up like Michael/Michelle or Christine Jorgensen, why not experience being locked up in a mental hospital? Going to a mental hospital was oversized and dramatic; it would be another chapter in my *tragique* arc. I would go to a hospital like the one in *Splendor in the Grass*, a movie I had seen eleven times in one week. It takes place in Kansas in the 1920s, and Deanie, Natalie Wood's character, is a repressed high school student who has a nervous breakdown over Bud, played by Warren Beatty, whom she so ached to sleep with. After her suicide attempt her parents send Deanie to a hospital that looks like a big old country house, with wide porches and rocking chairs, and a green lawn where patients can paint *en plein air*. Deanie's wise, fatherly doctor nurtures her back to health and stability. Of course, when Deanie gets out of the hospital two and a half years later, one of the first things she does is go to see Bud, to put it to rest. He has dropped out of Yale and married a greasy pizza restaurant waitress, played by Zohra Lampert, who has one little kid clinging to her dirty dress and another on the way. Deanie sees this and realizes it's over. As she's driven away from Bud for the last time—Bud so changed, Deanie so changed—she recites silently to herself Wordsworth's *Ode: Intimations of Immortality*, "What though the radiance which was once so bright / Be now forever taken from my sight, / Though nothing can bring back the hour / Of splendour in the grass, of glory in the flower / We will grieve not, rather find / Strength in what lies behind." I wept bitterly in the movie theater the first time I heard those words, reeling with the sense of loss, not even knowing why.

So when Dr. Doris suggested I go to a mental hospital, I figured I would be like Deanie, and it would be an adventure. A lark.

Before she could wheel herself out the door, I said, "I'll go."

I didn't have much else to do.

Marilyn Monroe

My father drove me home from the hospital in silence, the squeak of the windshield wipers in counterpoint to the sound of his deviated septum and the splattering of sleet on the windshield. We parked down the block from the store and I followed him up the street, staring straight ahead as we passed the windows of the Culver Luncheonette, the butcher, the deli, and Rose's, where the saleswomen stared at me from inside the store. We went behind the mirrored door in the lobby and up a gloomy flight of stairs to our apartment.

Things were pretty hushed in our house, what with me waiting to be put away. My mother made up a bed for me on the three-piece sectional sofa in the living room so I could watch TV. She turned on all the lights, but even with the lights on the room was moody. The apartment would have been a railroad flat except for an airshaft that we shared with Old Man McGlynn and a young Irish couple who never spoke to us in the street but who must have known everything that happened in our house, what with my father screaming all the time. They were our intimates more than anybody, yet I didn't even know their names.

That first day back in the apartment was scary, waiting for the phone to ring to say it was time for me to go to the hospital. I watched TV and dozed on and off, the ping of the knocking pipes familiar and comforting. Late that afternoon Dr. Doris called to say that a bed would be available for me at Hillside Hospital in Queens, where I should report at 9 a.m. the day after tomorrow. In Queens? I remembered that there was a hospital complex on a hill in Queens that I could see from the Long Island Expressway. But that couldn't be the hospital where I was supposed to go, because the hospital in Queens was a state hospital, a massive complex of glazed tan brick buildings, with bars on the windows. It must have held a thousand people. It was a *snake pit*, for God's sake, like the snake pit in the movie of the same name starring Olivia de Havilland, who was nominated for an Oscar for her role as Virginia Cunningham, a writer who wakes up in a mental hospital with drooling psychotics all over the place and she can't even remember how she got there.

I asked Dr. Doris if Hillside was the place near the Long Island Expressway, but all she would say was that it was a very good hospital, and I would get the help I needed there. So when Dr. Doris got off the phone, I got the number of Hillside from information and I spoke with a woman in admissions and asked her if Hillside was a tan brick building near the Long Island Expressway. She said it was. I asked if it had bars on the windows, and she said, "No, no. They're louvered safety windows." And did they have private rooms? "No," she said, "there are only dormitories, and a separate unit for adolescents."

It was like Oliver Twist. I would be locked behind louvered safety windows, sleeping in a dormitory with adolescent mental cases. This was *unacceptable*. I called Dr. Doris back to tell her I didn't want to go to Hillside, but I only got her answering service, so every fifteen minutes I called her service and left increasingly frantic messages until finally Dr. Doris called back, apoplectic. "*Why did you call six times?*" she demanded. I told her that I had called Hillside and she yelled, "*Why?*"

"Please, I don't want to go to Hillside!" I pleaded. "It's a mental hospital!"

"Nonsense!" She was snarling mad now. "You're going to be committed to Hillside tomorrow."

"*Committed?*"

"What did you *think* was going to happen?" she sputtered. "You're a minor! I want you to put your father on the phone *immediately*!"

"*He's not here!*" I shouted, and she hung up on me.

I sank to the floor in despair. What would happen? Would men in white jackets come and take me away, carry me down the stairs to an ambulance with everybody on 18th Avenue watching, the saleswomen clucking their tongues, Silverstein in the deli standing behind the hot dog griddle in the window calling his wife to come see the spectacle, Klenetsky standing outside his butcher shop in a bloody apron, scowling and shaking his head, like he knew it was bound to happen? And in the Culver Luncheonette, Arnie and Irv would be laughing with happiness. I would rather die than have Arnie and Irv laughing with happiness that I had come to no good.

So I decided that I would finish what I started. Later that night I would slip out of the house and throw myself under the D train, northbound to Manhattan, which I thought was more glamorous than throwing myself under a train headed to Coney Island. The trains ran only every half hour after midnight, so I could time it for about 2 a.m., when my parents would be asleep and the station deserted. It was only a one-minute walk to the elevated line, up a flight of stairs, the booth would be closed, and I could sneak under the turnstile. Standing up there I would be able to feel the vibration of the train at Avenue J, the stop before 18th Avenue, and I would turn toward the tracks and clench my fists and jump into the lights of the train as it pulled into the station. I would be crushed to pieces before I knew what hit me.

But once I started thinking about it, I realized it would be hard to do, jumping in front of a train. It made my heart beat wildly just thinking about it. Would death be quick? Instantaneous? Would I be dead before I knew it? Or would I just be mangled? Maybe I could electrocute myself on the third rail instead. Gog always warned me about the man who peed on the third rail and the electricity traveled up his urine into his penis and killed him. I could pee myself to death; that would give them something to talk about.

So when my parents went to bed, I wrapped myself in an old quilt over my street clothes and watched the time on the clock on the end table. As it got closer to 2 a.m I decided I would say *kaddish* for myself, the Jewish prayer for the dead. I didn't know what the words meant, but they were the only words I ever remembered from Jewish prayers. They were Aramaic, thousands of years old, and the prayer was especially beautiful because of the way the sounds kept repeating. *Yis-borach v'yish-tabach v'yi-spoar v'yis-romam v'yis-masay, v'yis-hador v'yis-'aleh v'yis-alal, shmay d'kudsho, brich hu . . . Blessed, praised, glorified, exalted, extolled, honored, elevated and lauded, be the Name of the holy one . . . Blessed, praised, glorified, exalted, extolled, honored, elevated and lauded, be the Name of the holy one. . .* I prayed for my parents, and for everyone I loved, and I even prayed for people who forsook me, like Lily Williams.

While I was doing all this praying the TV was on in the background, and I heard a man say that Marilyn Monroe was going to star in a new movie called *Something's Got to Give*, with the French actor Yves Montand, and that it was a remake of a screwball comedy from 1940 called *My Favorite Wife*. I got distracted by the Marilyn Monroe news and stopped saying *kaddish*. There was footage of Monroe with Tony Curtis from *Some Like It Hot*. A reporter said *Something's Got to Give* would be her first film since she was hospitalized the year before. Then they showed black-and-white footage of her looking frantic, wearing a coat with the collar pulled up, being jostled by a huge mob of reporters and photographers. She was trying to make her way through the hallway of a hospital. There was pure hysteria, the hot white bursts of flashbulbs going off like lightning, and she was petrified. The reporter said that after Monroe divorced the playwright Arthur Miller she had a "nervous breakdown," and that she had signed herself into the famed Payne Whitney Psychiatric Clinic of New York Hospital. They showed a picture of a formidable piece of real estate standing hard by the East River Drive, a stout, nine-story building with Gothic arches and small, screened windows. The announcer said that Payne Whitney was the "Ivy League of psychiatric hospitals," and it was so exclusive that only two hundred patients were treated there in a single year.

I didn't have to throw myself under a train. Nervous breakdown! That's probably what I had, a nervous breakdown, a wonderful expression that described the sort of despair and general hopelessness to which I was partial. What I needed was Payne Whitney.

Early the next morning I called the admissions office at Payne Whitney to inquire if they had private rooms with baths. The woman hung up on me. I called back and I begged her, "Please, this is no joke. They want me to go to a hospital called Hillside in Queens and I need to find out what it's like in Payne Whitney."

"How old are you?" she asked. When I told her I was fifteen she softened. "I can't say much," she said. "But you can't just call up and request a room—you need to be referred by a doctor."

"I understand," I said. "I *have* a doctor. But I need to find out, *are there private rooms?*"

"Payne Whitney is a hospital, not a hotel, and patients can't reserve a particular kind of room," she said. "But yes, there are private rooms."

"And are there bars on the windows?" I asked.

"No bars."

"This is good," I told her. She gave me the name of the admitting doctor and I wrote it down on a piece of paper. Then I left more frantic messages with Dr. Doris's answering service.

She sounded exasperated when she called back. "*What is it?*"

Without mentioning Marilyn Monroe, I told her that I would go to a hospital peacefully if it was Payne Whitney. I said that I had already called Payne Whitney and needed her to make the referral, and that Payne Whitney was the place I really wanted to go. I must have sounded like I was pledging myself to a sports team.

"Payne Whitney?" she asked incredulously. "The *temerity*! Don't you *dare* call any more hospitals! You have no say in the matter! You're going to *Hillside*."

"But why not Payne Whitney?"

"Because Payne Whitney is an expensive, private psychiatric clinic."

Expensive? Of course. I hadn't thought about money. I guessed Marilyn Monroe could afford it. "What if I can get my grandfather to pay for it?" I asked Dr. Doris.

"It doesn't matter! I *forbid* it. They can't give you the kind of long-term care you need."

There was a sudden silence on her end of the line, as if she had let something slip.

"Long-term?" I asked. "How long?"

"*Now you listen to me, young man!*" she said, raising her voice.

"This is *my life* you're talking about!" I shouted back, and I hung up on her this time.

Gog

Gog—the nickname I gave to him when I was a toddler—was sitting in the living room on one of the two gold brocade chairs my mother bought from Modern Living on Kings Highway. The winter sun had disappeared behind the elevated line, covering the room in shadows, and through the front windows I could see the Great World Chinese restaurant neon sign flickering on. Gog was ruminating about the marvels of modern engineering. He was wearing a striped suit, a dress shirt with no tie, and he dabbed at his watery blue eyes with a linen handkerchief. He was saying that the giant exhaust fans in the Brooklyn–Battery Tunnel were so big that they exchanged all the air in the tunnel every ninety seconds so people wouldn't get carbon monoxide poisoning, and wasn't it remarkable that in the middle of the heat of an automobile engine you could make air conditioning? The car show was at the New York Coliseum, he said, and he had just gone the day before.

"Boy-oh-boy," he said with glee, rubbing his hands together. "The new Corvettes are certainly beautiful. They're made of *plastic*. Plastic cars, Stevie, stronger than steel!" He was the only one who called me Stevie.

"Are you going to get one?" I asked.

"Without doubt," he said. "But if you ever wanted to see the *most beautiful car ever*, you should see the new XKE Jaguar." He said that the XKE looked like a bullet, and it was slung so low you rode in it with your feet out in front of you and your behind only inches off the ground. He loved cars, like I did, or maybe I loved cars because of him. Gog was so charming that, no matter all the flashy cars and girlfriends and Miami Beach suntans, everyone still adored him, including my mother and me and a whole harem of women in the store. Much to my father's consternation. Despite Gog's serial philandering, he had what my father wanted more than anything in the world—*koved*, it's called in Yiddish, honor and dignity.

Harry Goshinsky was a rake from the start, a Lower East Side boulevardier from Pinsk, a nineteen-year-old who cut a dapper figure in a black waistcoat and derby. Rose Yashinovsky, twenty, short and sturdy, was an old maid by the wisdom of the time, the homely daughter of a fishmonger from Bialystok. By the time Harry got my grandmother pregnant in 1923, he had bedded every decent-looking girl on Rivington Street. At first he refused to marry Rose, but after he was railroaded into it by her family, he grew to love her. They had two daughters, Ruth, my mother, and three years later another girl, Lamour.

Although Gog made only three dollars a day packing robes in the Garment Center, they were able to save enough to open a tiny yarn and knitting shop in a sliver of a storefront on 18th Avenue. Gog bought wool remnants in the Garment Center, a penny for five yards, and Rose tied together skeins of yarn to sell. She taught knitting for free to the neighborhood women, and the little store became a meeting place. In the winter, those who came to knit mittens for children were given free yarn, and in the summer, when it was too warm to knit, the women sat on wood kitchen chairs on the sidewalk "taking in the sun," while they traded gossip.

One day, in the winter of 1930, when people were jumping out of windows and living in Hooverville in Central Park, a customer told my grandmother a sad story about a fourteen-year-old orphan, a refuge from the Ukraine, who lived in a shack in New Jersey. Her parents had died of cancer a few months apart after arriving in the United States. The girl was left by herself to scavenge in a train yard for coal she could burn in a tin can to keep warm.

The story so touched Rose that although there was hardly an inch of space in their one-bedroom apartment, she offered that the unfortunate child could move in with her and Harry and sleep on a cot in the hallway, in exchange for helping her take care of the babies.

The Little Match Girl who showed up was Katherine Baralecki, a rosy-cheeked Slavic beauty with clear blue eyes. She had only the clothes on her back and a change of underwear in a sack. She seized her new opportunity with enthusiasm. She watched the children, cleaned the house, learned to cook kosher, and she was out of the cot and into my grandfather's bed in a matter of weeks while my grandmother taught knitting.

When it dawned on Rose what was happening she called Katherine "every name in the book," as she put it, and threw her out the door, despite my grandfather's feeble protests. Then my grandmother packed her own suitcase, tied it closed with rope, and took her daughters out into the street. She stood there shivering, wondering where to go, and when she couldn't think of any place, she went to the Culver Theater to keep warm. She sat in the dark, her petrified girls clinging to her, and she wept her way through six hours of double features and newsreels. When the theater closed that night, she resigned herself to taking the children home.

Rose was shocked when she returned to find Katherine sitting on the curb in front of the house. She marched past her, put the girls to sleep, and lay down in the darkness of her bedroom, next to her snoring husband. She lay awake for a while and then crept out of bed, went to the front door, opened it, and said, "Katherine, come in."

I don't know exactly how my grandmother managed to reconcile having Katherine in her life for the next fifty years, but she did; I guess they were like Jewish Mormons. Eventually Katherine became more than the tolerated mistress—she shared matriarchal duties with my grandmother. She held a position of authority and respect in our family. She helped raise all of us. She was the court of appeals for three generations. It was Katherine of the Ukrainian superpowers who walked in front of my grandfather's Biarritz in a thick fog on the Southern State Parkway, leading the way to Exit 21 with a flashlight. It was Katherine who carried a carved mahogany dining room table up a flight of stairs on her back with no help. And when no one would let me have a chemistry set because it was too dangerous, it was Katherine who overruled the veto and gave me the twenty bucks to buy it. I set myself on fire at the kitchen table, but that was beside the point.

Curious outsiders were told that Katherine was my grandfather's sister. She might as well have been, because their relationship turned platonic within a short time. Truth be told, Gog had two wives to deal with, not two lovers, and in later years Katherine got so bossy he nick-named her "the Sergeant."

The little knitting store began to sell ladies' stockings, and then underwear and gloves, and in the early 1940s my grandfather was able to buy a commercial building down the block with two apartments above it. He opened Rose's Bras Girdles Sportswear, with the name "Rose's" spelled out in pink neon script on the sign across the front of the building. The store fared well, benefitting greatly from Fleischman's gown salon down the block, where they sent customers to Rose's to buy custom-fitted undergarments every time they sold a dress.

In the 1950s my grandfather bought a split-level house in Freeport, right next door to the bandleader Archie Bleyer, whose recordings of "Hernando's Hideaway" and "Mr. Sandman" were on the Hit Parade. Gog treated himself to a succession of Cadillacs and Corvettes, and when he and my grandmother and Katherine rode together in one of his Corvettes with the top down, my grandmother huddled in the passenger seat in a babushka, while Katherine sat on the hump of the gear shift between them, stuck up into the air, being whipped by sixty-mile-an-hour winds, yet intrepid, an incarnate metaphor of their triad.

Herka

The afternoon before I was supposed to be committed to Hillside, sitting in the apartment above the store, Gog began to talk about what it was like when he was my age. When he was fifteen he lived in a tenement on the Lower East Side, one of those terrible buildings with thirty families where everybody was sick. Tenements were built of dry tinder and heated by woodstoves in the winter, death-traps that could go up in flames in a second. His cousin Shmuel was burned to death in one of those firetraps, he said, and they were always terrified when they went to bed at night. In the summers the Lower East Side was like a coffin, he said. There wasn't a blade of grass or even a tree, there was no way to cool off, no place to take a swim, except for the East River, which was polluted by the beef slaughtering plants a mile or two to the north. But they didn't know about pollution back then. On the hottest days the boys would strip to their underwear shorts and jump off the rotting pier into the murky water. Afterwards they lay down on the splintered wood dock to dry in the sun.

"One day," Gog said, "I was looking at myself in the mirror before going swimming, and I reached behind me and I felt a huge hump! I had a big bone sticking out of my back under the skin. I couldn't believe it. I was deformed. I never knew it before. I had a *herka*," he said, using the Yiddish word for hunchback. "So I stopped going swimming. No matter how brutally hot it was, I never went to the river. For many years I never went swimming. Until one day I confessed to my brother Aaron, and he looked at me like I was crazy. I had no *herka*. It was my own shoulder blade that I was feeling. Everybody's shoulder blade sticks out when you reach around to touch it. And all those years I could have been swimming." He shook his head and took a handkerchief out of his back pocket to dab his watery eyes. There was heavy silence in the room except for the hiss of the radiator behind the sofa.

I knew what he was saying to me. Whatever I thought was my hunchback, it was okay. I was okay. I wanted so

badly to thank him for his words, but I was too embarrassed to speak, so I stupidly just nodded in the gloom,
and he understood that too, probably.

"I will pay for Payne Whitney for you, if that's what
you want," he said, his voice gravelly. "For six months, but
no more. I had hoped that one day I would leave you that
money, and it hurts me to give it to you now, especially for
this purpose. But if you find peace, it will be worth it to
all of us."

Four

Seventh Floor

Mildred DeSantis roamed the hallways of the seventh floor of Payne Whitney like Ophelia searching for a way out of Elsinore, except instead of shadowy stone passageways lit with torches, there were bright hallways painted institutional green and overhead strips of ghastly fluorescent lighting in unbreakable plastic fixtures that cast shadows on our faces like we were gargoyles. The parapet was a double-locked, heavy oak door, and the omnipresent clankety clank of keys on key rings was a constant reminder that you were imprisoned with no way out, with people no less crazy than Ophelia.

There was a war going on in Mrs. DeSantis's head, the crazy part trying to kill the sane. She never spoke or made a sound, but evil spirits must have pursued her. She spent hours in locomotion, like some sort of macabre battery-powered toy, shambling along the hallway with her hands out in front of her like a begging dog, and when she reached a cul-de-sac she'd march in place for a few seconds in her Gucci house slippers until it registered that she was facing an obstacle. Then the tension would rise in her already taut body, and in a Kabuki-like ritual she would hike up her dress to her waist and expose her mons pubis while she elaborately rearranged her panties—

Jesus Christ what was that all about?

Mrs. DeSantis did the "Thorazine shuffle." Thorazine was a new drug at the time, developed by the French and used to treat everything from manic depression to uncontrollable hiccups. It controlled hiccups because the drug put patients into such a stupor that their bodies couldn't hic: it was the equivalent of a chemical lobotomy. Mrs. DeSantis's husband was the largest exporter of wine in Portugal, and when her daughters came to visit her on Wednesdays they arrived in a limousine that waited for them in front of the main building. The nurses helped her put on makeup in the morning, and her family paid for her hair to be done every week.

On my first day in Payne Whiteney I decided I would walk up and down the halls with Mrs. DeSantis. I thought perhaps she'd appreciate a friend who treated her like a regular gal. I helped turn her around at a dead end so she wouldn't do that grotesque thing with her panties. I asked her questions about where she came from, and about her daughters, but of course she never answered, just stared straight ahead with frightened eyes like she was looking into hell.

"What are you doing?" one of the nurses asked me as Mrs. DeSantis and I strolled by as if we were in the Easter parade. "I'm just walking," I told the nurse.

After about an hour of my chattering away at her, Mrs. DeSantis turned toward me and our eyes met. For a second I could see a flicker of the real Mrs. DeSantis, a woman of intelligence with the self-awareness of what was happen-

ing to her. She shuffled up close to me and extended the
bony forefinger of her right hand and tried to poke out my
eye. She went after me with all her strength. I dodged her
thrust, but her fingernail gouged out a small crater on my
left cheek that began to drip hot blood down my face. She
looked at me with triumph and started stamping her feet
in tribal cadence, first one foot and then the other, like a
little victory dance, and suddenly a shower of urine was
pouring down from between her legs. I jumped back because it was splashing on my shoes. Another patient down
the hall called out, "Uh-oh, Millie's having a meltdown!"
and the nurses came running.

One of the nurses washed the gouge in my cheek with
hydrogen peroxide and another nurse came to my room
and asked me what happened, and if I had disturbed her
or provoked her. I explained I did nothing except walk
with her, but I could tell they weren't sure if I was telling
the truth. The only reason I could think why she tried to
blind me was that I annoyed her with all those questions,
and maybe she didn't need a strolling friend, maybe she
needed to be left alone after all.

As for movie stars, Marilyn Monroe had long ago left
the building. The nurses refused to say what room she
stayed in and the closest to her movie-star aura I could get
was to sit in the phone booth from which she begged Joe
DiMaggio to transfer her to the more demure psychiatric
facilities at Columbia Presbyterian. Monroe signed herself into Payne Whitney under the name of "Faye Miller,"
and Faye didn't like being on the seventh floor, because
the craziest people in the hospital were on seven, a sort of
WASP Charenton overlooking Manhattan.

Monroe wrote to her acting coach, "I'm locked up with

these poor nutty people. I'm sure to end up a nut, too, if I stay in this nightmare. Please help me." She didn't do herself any favors when she smashed the glass on one of the bathroom doors because it was locked. "Outside of that," she wrote, "I haven't done anything that is uncooperative." In a letter to another friend, she reported, "Everything was under lock and key; things like electric lights, dresser drawers, bathrooms, closets, bars concealed on the windows—the doors have windows so that patients can be visible all the time, also the violence and markings still remain on the walls from former patients. They asked me why I wasn't happy there. I answered, 'Well, I'd have to be nuts to like it there.'"

Mrs. DeSantis was a lighthearted distraction compared to the very rich Chinese man from Hong Kong who had put an expensive antique gun in his mouth and pulled the trigger. Because the bullet was old he only managed to destroy the back of his throat and part of his tongue, and instead of being dead he wound up speaking a slobbering growl and eating only brown gruel fed to him by a private nurse at mealtime. He wept and moaned that he didn't want to live that way, and I had to agree with him, he was better off dead.

I would have gladly assisted in the suicide of Ludovic, a milquetoast cellist with the New York Philharmonic, who obsessively repeated the story of his wife Eleanora's fatal accident when she slipped and fell on the ice in front of the Beresford apartment building on Central Park West where they lived. In stentorian tones and grandiloquent speech, he repeated the sequence of events of his wife's death in a monologue worn down into a rut: how they were coming home from a movie, the night was cold and the moon was full, and the sidewalk was slippery. He had taken her arm, but as they approached the building he let go, and she fell and cracked her head on the pavement and died under the canopy before the ambulance arrived. Every time he got to the point, "Had it not been for the fucking hand of fate she could have stepped six inches to the left and missed the ice," he started to cry, his shoulders jiggling up and down, tears running down from behind his glasses. Once he composed himself he complained that he would have to sell the apartment because he couldn't stand to walk in and out of the Beresford and look down on the spot where she died. He was pathetic, but annoying.

Ludovic had a loyal fan, a woman in her twenties named Melon who had a wandering eye so you never knew where she was looking, a problem complicated by a nervous tic she had, moving her head back and forth as she spoke so that her ponytail swished from side to side, like a horse's tail shooing away flies. Melon was Ludovic's claque. She murmured the appropriate sympathies every time he told his story, creepily assuring him, "Never forgotten. Never forgotten."

Finally, after Ludovic's fifth telling in fifteen minutes, a skinny guy with squinty eyes sitting in a chair nearby, so twitchy he practically vibrated, observed with a bright, childlike innocence, "You just told us that story!"

"What *story*?" Ludovic demanded, incredulous, drawing himself up as if his cello solo had just been interrupted by a catcall from the audience.

"The story about your wife dying," the twitchy man said.

Suddenly, shockingly, the morbidly depressed cellist leaped from the sofa and grabbed the twitchy guy by his throat, shaking him like it was an Apache dance. The guy was so scared he didn't even put up a fight, his arms just flailed around at his side as he was strangled. In another second a nurse and a male aide pried Ludovic's hands away. Although smiling again now, the twitchy guy had peed in his pants, and he was hustled off to the bathroom to change.

The nurse asked Ludovic if he wanted to spend some time in the "Quiet Room," or would he agree to take a sedative and have a nap in his own room? The Quiet Room was for agitated patients, ye olde padded cell, where they most likely put Marilyn Monroe when she smashed the bathroom window. It had floor-to-ceiling panels of wadding on the walls and floor, and a mattress pad to sleep on.

Ludovic cocked his head and asked the nurse earnestly, "How can I live this life?" This was the real Ludovic speaking for the first time, not the mourner. "Sometimes, when you love someone as much as I loved her, you simply cannot go on. Truth is, I'm scared."

"Now, Ludovic . . . ," the nurse said gently, taking his arm. "We all suffer loss, and grieve, and learn to move on."

The male aide took his other arm, but Ludovic shrugged him off. "I'm coming with you," he assured them. "I'll do anything you say. But tell me first. She was *everything.* Sometimes we wanted to murder each other, but we were together *forty-one years.* We were intertwined. She was the mother of *my son who killed himself.* And she slipped. An ignominious death for such an elegant soul, no? She slipped away from me. That's how I lost her." His shoulders slumped. He was a husk again.

"Ludovic, come with us," the nurse said.

"Yes, shoot me full of sedatives," Ludovic encouraged,

allowing himself to be led off. "I just want to sleep and not wake up again into this fucking nightmare."

They took him to his room and gave him an injection and an aide sat with him until he fell asleep.

After Ludovic was led away Melon came up to me, cheery and bright, as if we had just run into each other at the PTA meeting. "I have a question," she said. "Now that you're institutionalized, do you think you'll be stigmatized forever? I mean, you're a *mental patient*. Personally, I don't want to be ashamed forever."

Quiet Room

Late in the afternoon my first day in Payne Whitney, scared and homesick, I wandered down the north hallway to get away from the other patients and discovered an empty lounge. It was dingy and dimly lit; the Naugahyde furniture looked like it came from a Greyhound bus stop. Its saving grace was the tall windows overlooking the East River, practically just below me, separated from the hospital only by the East River Drive, which was streaming with rush hour traffic. The river was a majestic force coursing by so close, powerful and rough. It was dark out and snowflakes were blowing around in the wind like ashes. There was a tugboat with strings of lights like a carnival booth, hauling a dirty tanker through the foamy chop. Across from where I stood the river was breached by Roosevelt Island, where the crumbling shell of an abandoned prison and lunatic asylum was covered in a caul of ivy turned brackish-green by the cold. All of this was dominated in size and beauty by the 59th Street Bridge ten blocks to the south, its triple crescents anchoring Manhattan to the borough of Queens and Long Island beyond.

Behind me I could hear the muffled sound of weeping from a room down the hallway. I would have gone to my room to take a nap, but our rooms were locked until after dinner. My room had a single bed with a metal headboard that looked like a castoff from the TB ward, and bolted to the floor was an old bureau with locked drawers, scratched up as though some maniac had clawed at it. What had I been I thinking? How did I ever imagine that this was going to be an *adventure*? Suddenly a wave of homesickness flattened me, and I started to quietly cry.

I heard a tiny voice say, "What the fuck?"

There was a retching sound, and when I looked harder in the gloom behind me I realized there was a sylph of a woman lying on her side on the sofa, white as a ghost. She was wearing pajamas and a hospital robe, and her knees were coiled to her chest as tightly as if she was doing a full pike from a diving board. Every minute or so she would release and unwind a bit and try to throw up into a green metal pan placed next to the sofa, but nothing came up.

She squinted at me and groaned, "You're only *ten fucking years old*. What the fuck is this, some fucking amusement park?" Her hands trembled as she unclasped them from around her knees.

"I'm *fifteen* years old," I corrected her.

"Fifteen. Big fucking deal. Jesus," she said. "Sit the fuck down, you're making me dizzy." I sat in a chair near her. "What the fuck are you doing here?" she asked. I gave her a bare-bones outline of the previous week. "Jesus, that's an awful, awful story," she said. "Fifteen years old. Jesus. What the hell was bothering *you*?"

I shrugged. "What's bothering *you*?"

"Well," she said matter of factly, "I was going into P.J. Clark's around three in the afternoon last Sunday, and that's about the last fucking thing I remember. On Wednesday they broke down my apartment door. I was so drunk the booze was coming through my pores instead of sweat. Anyway, three days is a long fucking blackout."

"I saw *Lost Weekend*," I said. *Lost Weekend* was a movie about an alcoholic writer on a weekend binge, starring Ray Milland, who won the Oscar for Best Actor. "So I kind of understand what a blackout is like."

"Sure you do," she said.

"My dad's father was an alcoholic," I offered, to show solidarity. She snorted. I asked what her name was and she said, "Ellen." I asked what she did for work, and she said, "Random House."

"Oh, I know Random House," I told her. "It's owned by Bennett Cerf, who is so witty on *What's My Line* on TV. My mother and I love watching Bennett Cerf, but our real favorite on that show is Arlene Francis, who was married to Martin Gabel, the film director."

"You're some piece of work," she said to me, her eyes closed.

I asked her what she did at Random House and she said, "Editor." I asked if that meant that she corrected mistakes and she said I should shut the fuck up. To show her how literate my family was I told her that my grandmother and I read everything that Sidney Sheldon ever wrote.

A nurse came down the hallways to check on us. There were a lot of nurses and they were always hovering nearby.

They all dressed in different white uniforms and caps, depending on what nursing school they went to. This one's cap looked like a charlotte russe topping fell on her head. Ellen pulled a crumpled pack of Parliaments from her bathrobe pocket, her hand shaking so violently she could hardly get the cigarette to her mouth. The nurse lit it for her because patients were allowed to smoke in the lounge but they weren't allowed to carry matches.

"How are you doing?" the nurse asked her.

Ellen said she felt like shit.

"It'll pass," the nurse said. "You'll be a whole lot better tomorrow." The nurse smiled at me and asked how I was doing.

"All right, I guess," I said. "I'm homesick."

"That's understandable," she said. "If you need to talk, I'm in the nurses' office."

When she was down the hallway out of earshot, Ellen whispered conspiratorially, "Don't tell the nurses *anything*. They're fucking *spies*."

"Who do they spy for?" I whispered.

"They spy for the doctors. They write down *everything* you say. It's called *charting*. They watch you and listen, and every three hours they go into their little office and they write down everything, and your doctor reads it at night. It's like getting reported to the principal."

"What happens if you get charted bad?" I asked her.

"They zap you," she said.

"Zap?" Like Aunt Rifka. Shock therapy. A terrifying thought. I never considered for a moment they might shock me.

"You don't know what you're in for, do you?" Ellen whispered. She saw how frightened I was and she was en-

joying it. "After they shock you they turn you into a fucking zombie with Thorazine, it feels like your brain is in a
fucking straightjacket."

"I'll refuse to take that stuff, and they're not going to
shock me," I said determinedly, but scared out of my wits.

"Got no fucking choice," Ellen said, taking a drag on
her cigarette so sharp I could hear the paper crackle. "Got
no choice about anything," she said. "Got no choice if they
decide to give you shock treatment. In the morning you'll
see people in the hallway strapped to gurneys, all doped
up, waiting to be brought to the shock room in the basement. You know how they do it? They put a rubber bit in
your mouth so you won't bite your tongue off, and they put
wet electrodes over your temples, and then they throw a
switch and *fry your fucking brains*. You don't remember a
fucking thing after that. It erases your fucking memory."

I was now so scared I couldn't breathe. Oh, I had made
a dreadful mistake. A *terrible* mistake. This place was dangerous to my health. The charade was over. I made everyone believe I needed to be here, and I didn't. It was a
hoax. "I don't belong here," I said, standing up, my hands
shaking so badly I crossed my arms to keep them still.
"I'm going to go home." If they took me home from camp
they'd take me home from here.

"Fat fucking chance," Ellen said. "You're a fucking
ten-year-old, you can't go anywhere."

"*I'm fifteen years old!*" I shouted, and stormed down
the hallway to the nurse's office, counting the steps up to
twenty to calm down. The nurse's office had a Dutch door
with the top open, and I banged on the bottom part with
my fist. I told the nurse who came to see what the ruckus
was that I had made a mistake, and that I didn't need to

be there. I demanded she call my parents and tell them to come and get me.

"But you just got here," she said to me sweetly.

There were two other nurses in the office behind her, sitting at desks filling out charts, and they smiled at me sympathetically. "Are you feeling homesick?" one of them asked.

"Why, are you going to write that down?" I snarled. "Are you *charting* me? Then write down that I insist you call my mother and father and tell them I want to go home."

"You'll have to ask your doctor about a phone call home," the first nurse said, a tone cooler.

Now I made a bad decision. I decided to behave like my father. I banged on the doorframe with my fist and said I would call the police and have all of them arrested if they didn't call my parents.

The second nurse scowled at me and stood up at her desk. She said I had to calm down, that I was upsetting myself. So just to show her who was boss, I kicked the bottom of the Dutch door and shouted, "*You will call my parents!*"

"Stop kicking!" the first nurse said firmly. So I kicked the door again, really hard, and again, and just then, out of nowhere, a male aide came up behind me and put his arms around me, like a hoop around a barrel. That was the worst thing anybody could have done to me at that moment, to clamp me down, but he was strong, and his hands were locked together in front of my chest. The nurse said, "Quiet Room," and they carried me kicking and screaming down the hall, the other patients gaping at me as I was dragged by and locked in a padded cell.

The Quiet Room smelled of disinfectant but it was

toasty warm. I threw myself around the room for a while, flailing around against the padded walls, and then, bruised and spent, I fell to the thick mat flooring and sobbed and drooled. Presently, I felt strangely calm and fell asleep. I didn't realize that during the struggle they had jabbed me with a shot of chlorpromazine, an industrial-strength tranquilizer. When I was asleep a nurse came in and put a pillow under my head and covered me with a blanket, and they checked on me every half hour and took my pulse.

The air in the room changed while I slept; the hot dry air from the radiator turned balmy and soft. The hospital was a hotel, and there were white stucco buildings and a huge blue sky, so much bigger than the sky in Brooklyn that the horizon curved, and the ocean was translucent. There were tiny umbrellas on the strawberry shortcake. I kept the umbrellas for years until they shredded and I threw them away. My mother rubbed suntan lotion on my face and there was that coconut smell again and she said that I had freckles like I did in the summer. There was a tiny windmill and you had to get your golf ball in the hole at the bottom in between the turning sails. Then it got scary because my father was screaming, a small, scratchy voice coming out of a black hammer, but the hammer was really a telephone and he couldn't get at us until we went home. My mother and I slept in a big bed together with ironed linens that smelled like coconut and Gog killed the pink balloons on the beach with a shovel, like bursting bubble gum. I was seven years old.

I woke in the Quiet Room. I lay still in the dark for a long time until I came to my senses, and then I wrapped myself in the blanket and went to the window. Eighteenth Avenue would have been deserted at that time of night, except for maybe a drunk stumbling out of McGlynn's. But Manhattan was lit up with people's lives. It was a clear, frosty night, and people hurried along the street with cars and many taxis, and smoking manholes like in the movies. I could see the windows of the buildings along York Avenue, lighted by the jumpy flashes of TV sets. Directly below me were the grounds of Rockefeller University, and if I pressed my head against the cold metal grating I could see a sleek, white, ultramodern house, which I later learned was the private residence of the president of Rockefeller University. There must have been some sort of a party breaking up because guests were leaving and a queue of limousines was backed up around a cobblestone drive surrounding a tiled fountain. The women were dressed in cocktail dresses and the men were wearing dinner jackets. This must be what life is like in Manhattan, I thought. It made me sad, because I would never wear a tuxedo to dinner or know that kind of people, and I would never know what to talk about over dinner, even if I ever got invited to one. I was in a padded cell.

At least, I consoled myself, this was the first night that I would sleep in Manhattan.

Wayne Myers

The resident who had been randomly assigned to my case by the clinic was named Wayne Myers, and his name was all I would know about him for many years to come. He was a tabula rasa on which I was supposed to imprint my own fantasies about him and facilitate transference, the cornerstone of Freudian analysis. But I knew none of that then.

All I knew was that when the door opened to the Quiet Room the next morning, I was hoping to find a wise, middle-aged doctor, like Lee J. Cobb in *The Three Faces of Eve*, who guides Joanne Woodward back from multiple personalities and helps her reduce all the people inside her into one healthy person, a role for which she won the Academy Award for Best Actress in 1957. Instead, a quiet-spoken, open-faced young man in a white lab coat showed up early in the morning and asked me if I had calmed down enough to go to the dining room with him and have breakfast.

"I heard you had a rough first day," he said, sitting at a table with me in the deserted room while I polished off watery soft-boiled eggs and cold toast. He had hooded blue eyes and a soft, laconic way of speaking that was calming. He wrote down almost everything I said on a yellow pad, a voluminous record that I couldn't imagine he would ever consult again.

"I made a mistake," I said, gulping down a glass of water with a shaky hand. "I'd like you to call my parents and ask them to come and get me."

"I see," he said, writing notes. "Can you tell me what happened last night that made you lose your temper?"

"I just want you to call my parents and tell them I want to go home."

He wrote that down and stared at what he had written thoughtfully. "I'll make a deal with you," he said. "I'll help you go home, but first you must convince me that you won't try to hurt yourself again."

"Okay, I won't," I said, with no great conviction.

"Why'd you do it?" he said.

"Attention," I claimed.

He nodded toward my bandaged wrists. "That wasn't

grandstanding," he said. He put down his pad and leaned back in his chair, balancing on its rear legs, like a kid in a college dormitory. "People looking for attention make some scratch marks, or swallow some aspirin, but you made a pretty serious attempt to kill yourself. Statistically, you're at risk for another try."

"I'm not going to try to kill myself," I said, with a trifle more conviction.

"Again," he said. I looked at him quizzically. "You're not going to try to kill yourself *again*," he said. "You tried once."

"Okay, *again*."

"I'm glad to hear that," he said, nodding. He seemed like a pretty sincere guy to me. "Are you still counting?" he asked.

"Who told you about *that*?"

"Dr. Milman."

"Oh, you spoke to that witch. What does *she* know? I only knew her ten minutes."

"She said that you had been saving things and touching things and counting for many years."

"That stuff stopped," I told him. "I only still do it sometimes when I get nervous."

"Oh? When did it stop?"

I told him the counting and touching had started to "fade away" a year or so before.

"It's unusual for that kind of behavior to fade away," he said, writing it down.

"Well, it did."

"And Dr. Milman said that your grandfather is paying your hospital bill?"

"He owns a successful bra and girdle store in Borough Park," I said. "And we're very comfortable."

"I see," Dr. Myers said, writing it down. "Still, this hospital costs a great deal of money," he said. "It would be a pity for you to waste your grandfather's money."

"I won't waste his money because it won't cost him more than one day, since I'm going home as soon as you call my parents."

"If I called your parents I would advise them against taking you home," Dr. Myers said. "You haven't convinced me you won't try to hurt yourself again."

"*I don't need to be here! I want to go home!*" I shouted, bursting into tears. "I'm not your prisoner!"

"No, you're not a prisoner," he said, unperturbed by my shouting, offering me a Kleenex from a neatly folded pile he kept in the pocket of his lab coat. I blew my nose resentfully.

"What were you thinking when you started to cry?" he asked.

"Nothing," I said.

"You can't be thinking nothing. The mind is always working, even when you're asleep."

"I don't remember what I was thinking," I said.

"Really? You can't remember what you were thinking a second ago that made you cry?"

I tried to remember why I cried. I cried because I missed everything about 18th Avenue. I even missed the salesgirls. Funny how you can miss almost anybody. Maybe not Arnie and Irv. I could never face them again, after being locked in a mental hospital. They probably knew about it: Lily would have told them when she went for her coffee break. It was probably all over the neighborhood. How could I ever show my face again? Maybe I could stay in the apartment above the store all day and only go out at night.

Who would be the least likely person I could miss? Manny, the fat kid from Ocean Parkway, who had a strange odor. What was that stale smell that came off him? Manny used to hold his cocker spaniel dog up in front of the mirror and repeat to it over and over, "The dog. The dog. The dog," to see if he could teach the cocker spaniel he was a dog. Manny sometimes came over to watch TV and we read the *National Enquirer* out loud. Back then the *Enquirer* was all about gore and bloody accidents. One issue there was a photo caption under a horrific auto accident, "Martha's brains, circled." Manny and I laughed for hours. Martha's brains, circled.

The *National Enquirer* had a weekly contest where they paid five dollars for the best letter, so I wrote them a fake letter and signed it with my grandmother's name. The letter was supposed to be from a woman who went to a funeral and was offended that the corpse was buried in a blue satin evening gown. The letter writer railed that all dead people should be buried in black shrouds. Manny and I laughed ourselves into a puddle. I was stunned when two weeks later my letter won the contest, and it was published under a banner headline "Bury 'Em In Black." I carried that page of the *Enquirer* around with me for weeks and showed it to everybody on 18th Avenue. It was the first time I was published. I guess Manny was a friend, although I didn't have any normal friends, even before I was counting and touching things, because I didn't play sports and my father wanted me home immediately after school was over, and he made my mother come fetch me every day and bring me back to the store so something bad wouldn't happen to me, like getting kidnapped or hurt in the schoolyard. He said that it was no big deal to be picked up from school; his own mother had followed him to school every day. They lived in an apartment in Brownsville, a tough Brooklyn neighborhood. We drove there once; it looked full of Jewish thugs, and he showed me the little apartment building in which they lived where he was born on the kitchen table. I couldn't picture my grandmother, Leah, on the kitchen table with her legs spread. Leah watched him go to school every morning, following him from the rooftops, hopping and jumping from one to another to keep an eye on him until he got to school safely.

"What are you thinking?" Dr. Myers asked gently.

I blinked back from my time travel. "I don't remember," I lied. He cocked his head dubiously, so I figured what the hell. "I was thinking about how when my father was a little boy, his mother jumped from one roof to another to keep an eye on him walking to school, to make sure he was safe," I said.

"She did?" the doctor asked. "Jumping from one rooftop to another? How'd she do that? Was she an acrobat?"

Um, how could she have done that? I heard it repeated so many times I never gave it a second thought. But now that he mentioned it, Leah was a portly woman who never jumped over anything in her life. How could she jump from rooftop to rooftop? It seemed odd.

"What did your father think was going to happen to you in the schoolyard?" Dr. Myers asked.

"That I'd be hurt, like he was."

"How was he hurt?"

"Another boy kicked him in the testicles. Something was torn. He called it a 'rupture.' I'm not sure what that is, but they had to take him to the hospital and replace it with tendons from a lamb."

"From a *lamb*?" the doctor asked.

"Yes," I said. "It was tendons, I think."

"But you can't transfer tissue from one species to another," he said. "Do you understand that you can't put tendons from a lamb into a human?"

"But my dad told me dozens of times. Whenever I was a little boy and I tried to climb up on his lap he always flinched, and said 'Ooops!' He made me climb up gently because of the operation he had when he was a kid."

"Did it ever cross your mind that perhaps your father had an erection and he was trying to hide it from you?"

I was speechless. "No," I said.

"Don't you think your father had erections?" he asked.

"No," I said stubbornly.

"And why were they afraid you'd be kidnapped?" he asked. "Were there kidnappings in your area?"

I didn't think so, I told him. But it seemed an imminent danger, the way my father rehearsed me for hours about what to do if a stranger tried try to abduct me on the street (I should scream and run away), or if someone that I already knew, like a neighbor, or a customer in the store, should show up on the street and lie that my parents were sick and they would take me to the hospital if I got in their car (I should scream and run away), and that only certain relatives could be trusted in case of dire emergency. "What if Uncle Harry comes to school and says the store burned down and to come with him, what will you do?" I was quizzed. (Don't go, make the teacher call the store.)

Dr. Myers cocked his head, rapt. Nobody seemed interested in what I had to say before and I was intrigued, so I went on. I told him that when I went to the Culver Theater on the corner they made me sit in the same seat, seventh row down on the left aisle. It didn't matter if the whole theater was empty, that was the only seat I could occupy; it was near the candy counter, next to the fire exit door in case of fire, and my mother would tip the matron to keep an eye on me. I was *never* to go to the men's room behind the projection booth. This was crucial, for scary reasons I couldn't quite understand. If I had to pee I was required to leave the theater and walk back to the store to use the bathroom.

"Curious they worried that all this harm might come to you," Dr. Myers said. "How did these precautions make you feel?"

Hmm. Suddenly it seemed unreasonable, all these precautions. "It made me feel scared," I said.

"I bet. How else?"

"I dunno."

"Special?"

I guess it *did* make me special, come to think of it. None of the other kids at school seemed likely to be re-paired with lamb tendon. None of the other kids were targets of some unspeakable horror that would happen to them in the movie theater men's room, nor were they im-portant enough that a kidnapper was coming for them. It wasn't as if my father was Charles Lindbergh, after all.

"It's interesting," Myers said, "that at the same time you were made to feel fearful, it also made you feel special in some way."

But I *was* special, wasn't I? Of course I needed pro-tection. *We* were special, the Goldberg-Gaines hybrid. At that moment something began to coalesce in my head. Our family was special among all the other families far and wide of 18th Avenue. There was some unspoken purpose to my life that was yet to be revealed. The counting, the crazy thoughts, they were all signs. Even if it *was* a horrible thing to be a homo, it made me unique. That horrible part of me also made me special. I saw the world differently. Maybe the way I saw it was askew from the way most people saw it, but I had a separate sensibility that only homos knew. In some convoluted way, this realization that my homosexuality gave me a gift was like the moment in the movie *The Miracle Worker* when Helen Keller realized that Annie Sullivan's hand symbol meant "water." My curse in some ways made me . . . superior.

Dr. Myers watched my expression as this train of thought played out in my head. Special. Different. Something I'd chew on for a long while. He had managed to pull off a clever psychological sleight of hand by producing epiphanies out of a hat. Self-examination with a good shrink is like an opiate.

"What are you thinking?" he asked me.

"What are *you* thinking?" I challenged him, unable to suppress a small smile.

"I was thinking that you shouldn't go home," he said. "I was thinking that we can help you here, and that you're smart enough to benefit from analysis. I'd like you to hang in for another few days, at least until a bed opens up on a lower floor. You'll like the lower floors a lot better, there are many fewer restrictions, and the patients are healthier. But every patient who comes to Payne Whitney starts here on the seventh floor for observation. I'll help you get through this first week. We'll talk every day, and if you have an emergency you can tell the nurse and she'll come find me. But you can't lose your temper and kick things."

"Will you make me take medication and turn me into a zombie, like Mrs. DeSantis?"

He looked hurt. "Mrs. DeSantis is my patient, and she's not a zombie," he said. "You don't fit the profile of a patient who needs Thorazine, but if that was the best treatment for you, we'd talk about it."

"No. We're not even going to even talk about it. Because I'm telling you now. No zombie. And no shock treatment."

"Okay. You told me," he said. "So, do we have a deal?"

"One week," I said, holding up my index finger. "One week, and then I'm going home."

Five

Mr. Halliday

The third floor of Payne Whitney reminded me of the Beauregard, the small residential hotel in Bournemouth, England, in the movie *Separate Tables*. The hotel is a little worn, but clean and comfortable, with Irish lace window curtains. All the seemingly respectable, long time residents have secrets and surprises that reveal themselves over the winter. For instance, David Niven's character isn't really a major; he's a lonely man who had been arrested for feeling up women in the local movie theater. (Niven won the Best Actor Oscar for it in 1958.) And the hotel's manager, played by Rita Hayworth, is secretly engaged to Burt Lancaster's character, an ex-alcoholic. The people on the third floor of Payne Whitney had secrets like that. Only I think our peccadilloes were more interesting.

Three was only half a floor. There was a wall down the middle separating our side from twelve patients on the south side who were in an experimental six-month dietary study for which they ate the same exact meal three times a day—each portion weighed out to the gram so they had to eat every last scrap. The patients chose one favorite meal when they started the program. I tried to imagine what it would be like to sit down at breakfast for my ninety-fourth meal of shrimp in lobster sauce with house-special fried rice. We weren't allowed any contact with the patients in the study, and when I spied them walking in the manicured hospital garden ahead of us, or being herded into one of the large elevators, I wanted to try to slip one of them a stick of gum. What this dietary experiment achieved, I have no idea.

I was the only youngster with eleven adults on the third floor. Almost all the patients chain-smoked, and a layer of gauzy smoke collected a foot below the hallway ceiling under an unbroken line of ghastly fluorescent lights encased in a plastic shield. Audubon prints in plastic frames were screwed into the walls, in a smoking lounge with frumpy slipcovered sofas and a console television on which was glued a plaque that read "Donated by Arthur Murray." I was greatly impressed with Arthur Murray's generosity, but no one could explain why he would donate a television to a psychiatric hospital. I assumed he wanted crazy people to watch his show.

The night I was moved to the third floor I changed into a cocoa-brown pants and eggplant shirt ensemble before dinner and thought I looked very spiffy. A nurse brought me to a small dining room where the patients were eating dinner at tables set with white tablecloths and tiny ceramic vases with sprigs of flowers. If it weren't so brightly lighted it might have been an English tearoom. When I was ushered in by a nurse, the patients turned in unison to gape, a gallery of dour neurotics. Only one of them mumbled hello to me. An older man, with half-glasses down his nose and silver hair combed back like a bust of Beethoven, gave me a quick once-over and sneered, "Oh brother."

I guess he didn't know eggplant was the big color that season.

Ten minutes later I was seated at a table enjoying my dinner—pot roast, dumplings, red cabbage, and mashed potatoes—hunched over my food, eating like we always did at home, with the fork in my right fist and the knife in my left, when the white-haired man whispered sotto voce, "Barbara Ann," and everybody giggled.

I was crestfallen. Why was he calling me by a girl's name? I would mull this moment over in my mind for many years before it finally dawned on me that what he actually said was "barbarian." I guess I *was* a barbarian to them. I didn't eat like them, sound like them, dress like them, or behave like them. My clothing was the height of 18th Avenue fashion, and also they could see from the fresh wounds on my arms that I had clearly done something really nuts to myself.

After dinner I wandered down the hall to the main lounge where patients were watching television or playing cards. Off to the right there was a small, semicircular card room, dark and moody with all the lamps turned off except for a funnel of light from a low-hanging fixture over a card table. Lazy tendrils of smoke rose from a cigarette lying in an ashtray. Behind the table was a tall, elegant, middle-aged man, wearing pleated tan slacks and an ivory silk shirt buttoned to his neck, like a Mandarin. He was lost in thought, staring at a jigsaw puzzle on the table before him. He was holding puzzle pieces in his hand, caressing them as if to memorize their shapes. Behind him was an apse-shaped wall of leaded-glass windows overlooking the busy East River Drive, the passing automobiles streaks of headlights and taillights on the highway.

I must have been staring because without looking up he said testily, "Well, come in. It's rude to stand there gawking." I walked tentatively into the card room and introduced myself. He said his name was Richard Holiday.

"I never met anybody whose name was 'holiday' before," I said.

He made a short "Hah!" laughing sound, like I had amused him. "That's what Mother thought when I introduced myself—that my name was 'Holiday.'"

He was speaking gibberish, I thought. He picked up his cigarette from the ashtray and inhaled deeply before putting it back. "Take some puzzle pieces and make yourself useful," he ordered, exhaling a plume of smoke. I took a few pieces from the pile on the table and pretended to be looking for a fit. "This is a thousand-piece puzzle Mother sent to me," he said. "The nubs are almost all the same. It's better to concentrate on the picture and color of the piece, not the shape."

His mother must be very old, I thought. He had a twangy accent, like a western drawl, so I asked, "Are you from Texas?"

"Why, do I sound like a cowboy to you?" he grumped. "I was raised in Denver. I suppose that's the West."

"I'm from Brooklyn," I offered.

"Hmm. And we both wound up *here*!" he said, gesturing at the room. "The loony bin is the great leveler." He nodded at my bandages and asked if I had been in an accident, but I think he surmised what they were about. I gave him a brief rendition of my misadventures with the windowpanes, during which he interjected occasional "Oh my!"'s and "My Lord!"'s without actually taking his eyes off the puzzle. "There is a woman on this floor whose name is Letty," he said, "and she took a bottle of pills and passed out on her bathroom floor with her leg underneath her, and when she woke up three days later she was lame. Now she's got a lame leg to remind her for the rest of her life about her failed suicide."

"I guess I'm lucky nothing like that happened to me."

He gave me a sidelong glance. "But it *did* happen to you," he said, tightening his lips.

It took a second for this to sink in. People would see the scars and know. The mark of *come to no good*. Suddenly shame and regret for trying to kill myself filled me so profoundly I began to tremble. How would I ever be able to face anyone, to return home and see Lily and Katherine and Arnie and Irv? Mr. Holiday realized I was about to cry and said softly, "Now, now. Whoever said you have to lie in the bed you make was a fool. People are forever escaping their own caprice, and you will too." He gave me an encouraging, albeit brief, smile. "Here, help me with this puzzle," he said, handing me a sky-blue piece. "Take this piece and put it there." He touched a spot on the puzzle. Miraculously, it fit.

"What's this puzzle of?" I asked.

"It's Van Gogh's bedroom at Arles. Do you know what that is?"

I had seen the movie *Lust for Life* twice at the Culver Theater with Kirk Douglas as Van Gogh, for which he was nominated Best Actor, so I told Mr. Holiday that Van Gogh was an artist who cut off his ear.

"You're right," he said, nodding. "He was an artist who cut off his ear. He also lived for a time in a city called Arles, in France, in a rented house they called the 'Yellow House.' He painted his bedroom, many, many times. It was in Arles that he cut off his ear. Why do you think he cut off his ear?"

"For attention?" I guessed. "Because nobody was buying his paintings?"

"Nobody hurts themselves just for attention," Mr. Holiday said, eyeing me. "People hurt themselves because they're *nuts*. Van Gogh was nuts. To wit, he painted his own madness. A self-portrait with a bandaged ear that only a madman could paint. Don't you wish that you could paint your own madness?"

I didn't understand any of that, but I didn't want him to think I was stupid so I nodded.

"You know what they did with Van Gogh when he cut off his ear? They put him in a mental hospital."

"I never knew that."

"Of course you didn't."

"Why are *you* here?" I asked him.

"That's a rude question," he said.

"But I told you—"

"You told me *nothing*," he said, cooling. "You told me you did something stupid, is all you told me."

His mood had soured so much I thought perhaps I should leave, but then a nurse appeared in the doorway holding an elegant floral arrangement in a basket woven of green saplings. The flowers looked like they were made of tiny pieces of confetti glued together, baby blue and pink and mint, and some of the flowers were a maroon so dark the petals were like black velvet. The basket was tied with emerald grosgrain ribbon and a bow, to which was stapled a small white card. "Someone has sent you flowers," the nurse said cheerily to Mr. Holiday. I was enthralled. It was *so* glamorous to receive flowers in a mental hospital. I wished somebody would send me flowers. Who could I enlist to send me flowers? Fat Anna?

The nurse put the flowers down on the table but Mr. Holiday hardly gave them a glance. He went right back to his puzzle.

"What kind of flowers are they?" I asked.

"Bach-elor Buttons," he drawled.

"Bachelor Buttons," I repeated. Bachelor Buttons. "Aren't you going to open the card?"

"You *are* annoying," he said to me, snatching the envelope from the arrangement and opening it. "They're from Dick Rodgers," he said. "It says, 'Come home soon.'" He made a sour face and tossed the card on the table. "He's a little prick," Mr. Holiday said, going back to his puzzle. "He was in Payne Whitney himself, and I sent *him* flowers, and I wrote a note that said 'Come home soon.' Only I didn't mean it and he doesn't mean it either. He'd love for me to rot here." Mr. Holiday narrowed his eyes at me and asked, "Do you know who Richard Rodgers is?"

"A famous composer?"

He took a deep breath. "Richard Rodgers is one of the *great* geniuses of the American musical theater!" he said. "He wrote *The Sound of Music*! *The King and I*! *Carousel*! *South Pacific*! And he wrote incredibly beautiful songs, like 'My Funny Valentine'! He's also nuts. *Nuts*. He's seeing *five* psychiatrists, and none of them know about each other."

"How do you know Richard Rogers?" I asked.

Mr. Holiday drew himself up and looked down his nose at me. "How do I know him? I produced those shows."

"Oh, I didn't know . . ." I said, wide-eyed. Maybe this man was delusional. It was a mental hospital, after all.

"You don't know anything," he said, going back to his puzzle. "You don't even know how to hold your silverware. I saw you in the dining room tonight." He took a long drag on his cigarette and exhaled dragon smoke at me.

"I know how to hold silverware," I protested feebly.

"Do you know who my wife is?" he demanded. I shook my head. "My wife is Mary Martin. I hope you know who that is."

I was astonished. "Mary Martin who is Peter Pan?"

"Mary Martin who is Peter Pan," he mimicked me.

"I don't believe you," I said. When I was nine years old I became possessed when my mother read in the newspaper that the Broadway production of *Peter Pan*, starring Mary Martin, was going to be telecast live from a studio in Brooklyn, just two miles from where we lived. I made my father drive slowly past the studio building every day for weeks, staring at the bricks as if I had x-ray vision. For days leading up to the broadcast I could neither think nor talk of anything but Peter Pan. I watched the show lying on the floor of the living room in front of our black-and-white console TV, swooning and slack-jawed as Mary Martin and the Darling children glided clumsily through the air on thick cables.

"You don't believe me, do ya?" Mr. Holiday took a slim leather wallet from his back pocket and slipped a photograph out of a sleeve. "Here's a picture of Mother and me with Heller." It was a matte black-and-white photo of him and a woman who might have been Mary Martin, I wasn't sure, and a teenaged girl, standing in a farm field with mountains in the background. I was confused. He called Mary Martin "mother," and yet she was his wife? Maybe show business people called each other "mother" and "father"? Then it began to dawn on me. Unless this man was totally crazy, he was married to Mary Martin who was Peter Pan, and he was a famous Broadway producer.

I choked on my own saliva. I could have passed out from excitement. Perhaps he would discover me and put me in a Broadway show. I would be famous. I would be vindicated for being crazy. I could hold my head up. Even Arnie and Irv would have to show respect. I was so thrilled that when I tried to speak I gushed whatever came into my head. "I saw *Peter Pan* on TV three times," I said. "It was the best thing I *ever* saw on television. I know all of the songs by heart. The television studio was near my house in Brooklyn. And last year my parents took me to a Saturday matinee of *The Sound of Music*. It was *great*!"

"Well, that's very nice," he said stiffly, as if he was tired of hearing praise now that I was impressed. "You're a *faaan*," he drawled, grabbing a fresh handful of puzzle pieces. "That's what you'll say when I introduce you to Mother—'I'm a fan, and I saw *Peter Pan* three times, and I saw you in the *Sound of Music*, and you were *greaaaat*.'"

Introduce me to her. Had he said that?

He fell silent now and frowned, lost in dark rumination. "A good exit is even more important than a good entrance," he said to me. "An exit is the last impression a person has of you. More important I think than first impressions, because you can always change a first impression. But once you say goodbye, the court of appeals on you has closed. One of Mother's most important exits on stage was at the end of the second act of *South Pacific*, when Nellie says goodbye to Emile. Just before she exited stage right Mother hesitated for a brief moment—half a gesture, very subtle, ever so touching—and when the curtain came down everybody had tears in their eyes. Then one day after the show Noël Coward, that vile man, came backstage and said to Mother, 'How *wonderful* that exit was! The brief moment when you paused was superb.' And you know what? Mother was never able to make that exit again. Every time the moment came at the end of the second act she thought of what that prick Noël Coward had said to her, and her timing was off. He made her self-conscious, that evil man."

I guess I looked bewildered. "You don't know what I'm talking about, do you, Mr. Brooklyn?"

"I do. I think I do," I said, desperately not wanting to be Mr. Brooklyn, even though I had never heard of Noël Coward.

"I think now it's time for you to make *your* exit," he said. "I'd like to be left alone with my puzzle."

"Sure," I agreed, backing out the door like a geisha. "Will I see you tomorrow, Mr. Holiday?"

"We're locked up together," he said, dry as toast. "We have no *fucking* choice but to see each other tomorrow. And stop calling me 'Holiday.' My name is *Halliday*."

Halliday. Halliday. I floated down the hall on a cloud of stardust. Halliday. I must have looked like Butterfly McQueen in *Gone with the Wind*, lollygagging down the street waving her apron. Outside the nurse's office I ran into the woman who had been sitting at the table with the "Barbara Ann" man. Her name was Hilda, it would turn out. She was a Seven Sisters spinster recovering from a wee nervous collapse, a prickly soul who smelled of lavender. She had gray ringlets across her forehead like a flapper, and she was wearing a flannel bathrobe and men's pajamas. She owned a small savings and loan in Vermont and shoplifted at Bergdorf Goodman. Hilda carried a purse with her everywhere she went—hence her nickname, "Miss Moneybags"—although according to rules she wasn't allowed to have money in it. She had just taken her evening medications from a small paper cup while a nurse watched, so she didn't hide them under her tongue. "So you met Mr. Halliday?" she asked me with a mean smile. "Did he talk nonstop about Mary Martin?"

As far as I was concerned he could talk about Mary Martin all day and night. "No," I lied.

"He will," she assured me. "He *is* Mary Martin."

It turned out she was right, after a fashion.

Richard Halliday was consumed with being the husband, manager, producer, collaborator, costume consultant, and alter ego of Mary Martin. A former drama critic for the New York *World Telegram*, he married Mary Martin when she was a Hollywood ingénue and he was the story editor at Paramount Pictures, in an era when the story editor had the power to choose which films would be made. But Mary Martin somehow never really made it in pictures, and they gave up Hollywood for Broadway, where for the last thirty years of his life Mr. Halliday worked to turn her into one of the great stars of the American musical theater.

I became Richard Halliday's handmaiden. Every minute of the day I found some excuse to be near him, to sit next to him in the dining room or stand nearby in the elevator as we were shuttled up to occupational therapy, where I sat across from him as we wove raffia baskets. In retrospect I think the Archduke of Neverland felt reduced by the adulation of a rube kid, and yet he couldn't help but be flattered. Moreover, I was his only friend. Halliday didn't like the other patients, and they didn't seem to like him. He was mysterious. He never talked about his problems and kept mostly to himself, either reading or doing his jigsaw puzzles.

He was particularly at odds with Harold Kellogg, the "Barbara Ann" man from my first night in the dining room. The dapper Mr. Kellogg was a professor of architecture at Harvard, where he helped design the business school library, as well as libraries for Princeton and Cornell, and worked on over two hundred townhouses in Manhattan. He was also a dyed-in-the-wool anti-Semite and an insufferable snob who wore beautiful Scottish wool tweed sport jackets. Three months earlier he had written a letter to a colleague saying that he was going to hang himself in the library he had helped design. His family hustled him into Payne Whitney, where, instead of giving him shock treatment, lest the great architectural musings in his head be erased, the doctors put him on a new drug called Imipramine, the first of the tricyclic antidepressants. What they didn't realize was that Imipramine would swing Kellogg into a full-blown manic episodes. He started out the beginning of the day in a three-piece suit and ended it in a four-point restraint in the Quiet Room. They kept him on the seventh floor for a month before they were able to stabilize him. Once he came around, he was insufferable.

Kellogg didn't think much of Mr. Halliday, or the musical theater. If the two of them had been less gentlemanly, there would have been fisticuffs. As it stood there was a silence between them that frosted the air when they were in the same room. One day at lunch Kellogg proudly announced that the last Broadway show he saw was *Antigone* in 1946. I could see how this made Mr. Halliday steam. Out of Halliday's earshot, I heard Kellogg say that perhaps Mary Martin could teach Mr. Halliday how to fly. He also carped to the nurses that Mr. Halliday had appropriated the card table in the sunporch for his jigsaw puzzles while Kellogg and his bridge-playing cronies had to play on a rickety foldout table in the lounge.

I was happy to be Mr. Halliday's entourage of one, and we passed many winter afternoons together in the sunroom chatting while we assembled Van Gogh's bedroom at the Yellow House. He told me how Ezio Pinza's Italian accent was so bad during rehearsals for *South Pacific* that they had to teach him to say the words phonetically, and how Mother broke her elbow in two places and almost broke her back learning to fly during rehearsals of *Peter Pan*, and how horrible Noël Coward was to work with in London on *Pacific 1860*.

In turn I told him about making meat sauce with Tina Mastriano and the big dick on the donkey. I told him about the tribulations of trying to fit a double-D breast into a double-C cup when you didn't have the right size in stock. "You'd stuff in one side and the other side would plop out," I explained in earnest. I told him how Katherine came to live with us. At first he just tolerated my dotty Brooklyn stories, but over time he started to listen. He enjoyed a good tale. I was no Scheherazade, but he was a captive audience, and my stories were authentic pieces of a place deliciously foreign to him, with no passage there by any other conveyance than me.

"You should write all this down," he told me one afternoon.

It was just an offhand comment but I jumped on it hungrily. "Do you think I should? Really?" I prodded. "It's funny that you mention it because I was thinking of writing it down."

"I think you should," he nodded.

That's what I'll do, I told myself. I'll write them all down and publish them and then I'll be famous. But the next day I admitted to Mr. Halliday that I didn't know how to write them down. "Starting is the hardest part," he lectured. He was so right; it was a lifetime before I actually got around to it.

Splendor in the Grass

Payne Whitney might have been the Ivy League, but it was still a mental hospital and our days were regimented. We were expected up at 7 a.m., in bed by 10 p.m. We changed our sheets and made our own beds. We were expected promptly at meals when the dining room chimes rang at 8 a.m., 12:30, and 6:30 p.m. If you were ten minutes late to a meal you were charted and given a sandwich in your room. The nurses took our temperature and blood pressure every three hours and checked on us through the night. Patients from different floors were segregated from each other and they were moved around in groups, herded into the large elevators to be taken up to occupational therapy in the mornings or after lunch down to the formal garden with an octagonal path on which we walked round and round, gossiping about the other patients and our doctors. The only thing that took precedence over our daily schedules were sessions with our psychiatrists, which were held in our Spartan rooms in chairs facing each other.

At night, after dinner, we were brought to a gloomy institutional gymnasium that hadn't been renovated since Mr. Payne Whitney gifted the money to build the hospital. Kafka couldn't have created a more depressing landscape than the dimly lighted gym on the roof of the loony bin—although the views of the East Side of Manhattan and the 59th Street Bridge were exquisite. There wasn't much exercise equipment in the gym except for a sagging, shoulder-high net that did double duty for badminton and volleyball. I discovered that I liked volleyball, although it wasn't much of a challenge playing against Miss Moneybags. Still it was the first sport I kind of got.

There was also an ancient wood rowing machine that I began to use every night, rowing myself to nowhere fast, and one of the male aides taught me how to do sit-ups by hooking my feet under the calisthenics bar attached to the wall. With the stingy servings of hospital food and going to the gym every night, I began to lose my baby fat. Once I noticed the change in the mirror, vanity stirred in me, and I stopped eating bread and dessert.

There were only a few other adolescents, about whom I had no curiosity, only discomfort. I saw them in passing as we were transported up and down in the elevators. We stared at each other like caged animals recognizing their own species. They all looked crazy to me in their odd ways—a spooky squint, a strange tilt of head—and I didn't want to be sick like them. I wasn't, of course, because I was in some sort of a movie, and my craziness was only part of a series of plot twists, the latest of which was meeting Richard Halliday.

The first couple of weeks in therapy I talked nonstop about Mary Martin to Dr. Myers. My newly acquired encyclopedic knowledge of her career, filled with anecdotes about costume changes, so exasperated him that he finally told me to stop talking about her altogether. He said I was using it as a defense instead of talking about things that really mattered, that I should let myself free-associate and my mind wander. He just didn't understand. I couldn't stop talking about Mary Martin. I was a Lost Boy and she was Peter Pan. But instead of talking about Mary Martin, the usual suspects began to flicker across the screen: Aunt Rifka, Fat Anna, Katherine, Tina, and Little Rich.

Dr. Myers wrote it all down on his yellow pad like I was some oracle, but he reacted to nothing. Freudian analysis is Socratic, so if I asked him a personal question like, "Where are you from?" he would answer, "Where do you think I'm from?" And if I said I thought he was from New York, he'd ask, "What would it mean to you if I was from New York?" Cute. But I needed to know some basics about him to be able to communicate. Like, was he Jewish? Because Myers was a Jewish name. So when I asked if he was Jewish, he said, "What would it mean to you if I was Jewish?"

I said, "You would understand me better, and Myers is a Jewish name."

"It depends on how it's spelled," he said. I guess he meant Meyers, with two *e*'s. So, he wasn't even Jewish? How would he understand *anything*?

"What are you thinking?" he asked me.

"I'm thinking that you won't understand anything because you're a *goy*."

"How would you feel about that?"

It was infuriating.

Although it led to unexpected places.

One day I told him about my Borough Park *shtetl* and what it was like to have the Culver Theater on the corner. I told him about Murray the manager, and believing that I won the Schwinn bike, and that I could watch movies all day if I wanted. I probably watched hundreds of movies over the years, maybe thousands. I told Dr. Myers that I loved science fiction and horror, and any kind of family melodrama. Paddy Chayefsky was my favorite screenwriter. His situations were always so powerful and poignant, like in *Marty*, the film about a lonely, middle-aged Italian butcher from the Bronx, played by Ernest Borgnine, who won the Oscar for Best Actor in 1955 for the title role. And of course I told Dr. Myers about my favorite movie of all time, *Splendor in the Grass*, that I watched eleven times in six days. It was written by another great storyteller, William Inge, who won the Academy Award for best screenplay, as well as the Pulitzer Prize for writing the play and movie *Picnic*, that starred—

Dr. Myers roused from a long period of silence and asked, "What made you want to see *Splendor in the Grass* eleven times?"

"I don't know," I lied, flustered. The truth was that there was a shower scene in *Splendor in the Grass* in which you got to see Warren Beatty with his shirt off, and behind him was another guy in a towel, as erotic as any porn movie to me.

"I've seen that movie," Dr. Myers said. "The girl in that movie has a nervous breakdown."

"Yes," I said. "Deanie. Played by Natalie Wood."

"And she goes to a hospital?"

"Yes," I said.

"Like you?"

"I . . . guess so."

"Do you remember *why* she had a nervous breakdown?"

"Her mother—"

He interrupted me, breaking protocol. "She had a nervous breakdown because she wanted to have sex with her boyfriend, but sex is forbidden because she's a 'good girl,' and her mother wants her to be a virgin. And her bottled-up desire eventually drives her to a suicide attempt."

I felt my cheeks go on fire.

Dr. Myers asked, "What are you thinking?"

"Nothing," I said.

"You can't be thinking nothing."

I said, "I was thinking that I saw *Splendor in the Grass* eleven times because it was a very good movie."

Dr. Myers gave me a disapproving look, another breach of protocol, so he must have been really annoyed. "I need you to do this *with me*," he said. Then he announced the session was over, ten minutes early.

His displeasure unnerved me more than I expected. I was afraid he would stop caring about me. That night I asked Mr. Halliday if he lied to his psychiatrist, and he said that everybody lied to their therapist a little, but that it was a waste to lie because it was the doctor's job to make you better.

But what could I do? I couldn't bring myself to say that I saw *Splendor in the Grass* eleven times because I was in love with Warren Beatty. I lay awake in bed that night worrying. If I didn't tell him, then who would I tell? I tried to sleep but I had an erection that only a fifteen-year-old kid can have, and I finally broke down and masturbated, thinking about the lawnmower boy. When I was done I was more miserable than ever, ashamed and degraded. So I got out of bed and put on my bathrobe and went to the nurses' station, where I asked for a piece of paper and an envelope. I sat at the desk in my room and as Lana Turner tears of self-pity rolled down my cheeks, I wrote, "I THINK I AM A HOMOSEXUAL" in capital letters, signed it, sealed it in the envelope, addressed it to Dr. Myers, and walked leadenly down the hall with it in my hand. I forced myself to put it in the mail slot at the nurses' station before I could change my mind.

I dreaded seeing him at my regular session the next day, but he never brought it up. Nor the following session. Maybe the nurses had lost the envelope? Then finally, at the third session, I asked, "Did you get the letter I sent to you?"

"Yes," he said. I studied his face but there was nothing. "I thought I'd wait for you to bring it up when you felt comfortable talking about it."

I welled up. "I hate myself," I whispered. "I'd rather die than be one."

"I see," he said. "Is that why you tried to kill yourself?"

"I guess so." Okay, I finally admitted it to someone. But no great weight was lifted from my shoulders. To the contrary, there had been a kind of nobility in not telling that was now lost.

"Can you tell me why you think you're a homosexual?"

"I have feelings toward men."

"What kind of feelings?"

"Sex feelings."

"Have you ever acted on these feelings?"

"No."

"How long have you had these feelings?"

"I don't know. I think I always had them, before I knew what they were, but they turned different a couple of years ago."

"Different how?" he asked.

"The feelings got stronger."

"Did the feelings get stronger about the time you started counting and taking things?"

I thought of Camp Lokanda and wanting to go chest to chest with Brucie Cohen.

"Is it possible that in trying to repress those new sexual feelings, the only way for you to cope was to invent magic rituals like touching things, and saving things, which would momentarily alleviate the anxiety? You were probably like a pressure cooker trying to keep your feelings in. It was like trying to plug up a volcano. And it manifested itself in obsessive behavior."

He let that sink in for a moment.

"But why am I a homo?"

"Do you know anybody who's homosexual?"

"You mean like Christine Jorgensen?"

"Who?"

"Christine Jorgensen. He's a homo, isn't he?"

"I don't think so," Dr. Myers said.

"So why did they change him into a woman, if he wasn't a homo?"

"Christopher Jorgensen wasn't homosexual. He wanted to become a woman for another reason—because he didn't feel right being in a man's body. Is that how you feel? That you've been born in the wrong body?"

"*No*," I said, feeling insulted. "I feel like I've been born into the wrong *world*."

"Homosexual men don't usually become women."

"Yes they do," I insisted. "Or dress in women's clothing."

"No, they don't. Most live as men," he said. "Why do you say 'homo'?" he asked.

"That's what they're called, isn't it?"

"No, not really. It sounds mean the way you say it. I prefer to say 'homosexual,' which means 'same sex.'"

"I thought it meant 'men sex.'"

"No, it doesn't." He considered me as if he was trying to make a decision, and then, like he was confiding in me, sharing a great secret, he leaned forward and said, "You know, homosexuals can change. They can become heterosexual."

I was bewildered. "How?"

"I know men who were once homosexual, and now they're married and have children," he said.

"You?"

"No, not me. But other doctors."

"Does that mean they stopped being attracted to men?" I couldn't imagine.

"Absolutely," he said. "Homosexuality can be cured, like many other disorders. The key thing is, it's a tough row to hoe, and you have to *really* want to change."

Of course I really wanted to change. If it was possible for me to become normal, then why not? The world wouldn't be inside out, my whole life wouldn't be a sham. I could hold my head up. I could marry and have children, and nobody would be ashamed of me. I could listen to love songs on the radio and understand what it meant to be in love with a woman. I would jump through *hoops of fire* if I could be normal.

"Yes, yes," I said. "I really want to change."

"Then we'll begin next session."

Later that afternoon, when I went to work on the puzzle with Mr. Halliday, I was grinning like the Cheshire cat. "Okay. Spit it out," he said. "You look like you're bursting to tell me something."

"I told Dr. Myers that I was a homosexual," I said, hoping to shock him.

"Good for you!" he cheered, not seeming surprised at all. He pretended to busy himself with his jigsaw while he waited for me to say more.

"Aren't you surprised?" I asked.

"At what?"

"That I'm a homosexual."

He looked at me for a moment and said, "Yes. I'm shocked."

"Did you know that homosexual means 'same sex,' and not 'man sex'?" I asked.

"How *fascinating*," Mr. Halliday said. "And what did your doctor say when you told him?"

"He said he was going to fix it."

"*Fix it?*" Mr. Halliday asked, his voice rising. "How is he going to fix it? Does fixing it take longer than cooking a *cassoulet*?"

I said I didn't know what a *cassoulet* was, and it didn't matter how long it took. I was hurt by his skepticism. Although, he did raise an interesting question. How long was it going to take to become heterosexual? I promised myself I was going to look up *cassoulet* in the dictionary as soon as I could.

Cassoulet

Once we got down to work it turned out that Dr. Myers believed a whole lot of confusing things. Sometimes he said that homosexuality was an arrested state of infantile development, and sometimes he said that I was trapped in an oedipal stage. Like Oedipus, he pointed out, I hated my father and wanted him dead, and unconsciously I equated having sex with women with having sex with my mother, which is why I was so adverse and fearful of heterosexuality. Yet he maintained I secretly wished my mother dead too. He said I unconsciously feared my repressed anger would kill her, which is why I counted and exhibited obsessive behavior. But I loved her, so why would I want her dead? And what did that have to do with making me desire men? And why didn't I desire women? I just didn't get it.

"Is that Freud?" I used to ask Dr. Myers skeptically, when he told me what sounded like some fantastic theory. Was it Freud that homosexuality can be cured? In fact, no. Freud held that homosexuality was a part of human nature, and not an illness. But I never asked Dr. Myers if curing homosexuality was Freud.

Dr. Myers said that the way I would get better was by knowing things about my life and why I held certain misbeliefs. Understanding the root of my problems would make them disappear. If you know your blindness is hysterical, you'll be able to see. If we discovered what made me homosexual, I wouldn't be one anymore. In addition, we were going to deny sustenance to the homosexual part of me while nourishing the heterosexual man that Dr. Myers assured me lurked within, a man who I had displaced, but who could be found and reanimated. To start,

Dr. Myers said, I had to stop thinking about boys when I masturbated. Every time I masturbated thinking about a boy it was "another brick in the wall" to my heterosexuality, he said. He suggested that I should masturbate thinking about women, a chore harder for me than he probably imagined. I didn't tell him about the lawnmower boy; it would have been a betrayal.

Dr. Myers wrote notes on the yellow pad, furiously scribbling away no matter what I said. Occasionally something would really pique his interest. When I told him about pulling open the curtains in the dressing rooms of the store to expose the unfortunate women being fitted for undergarments, he posited it might easily have given me a misimpression about the sensuousness of the female form. No doubt. He found it significant that in the store I usually heard of female organs described as "plumbing," as in, "Mrs. Brodsky had plumbing problems." The word "vagina" was never spoken. He wrote that down.

Dr. Myers thought it was especially significant that I witnessed the incident when the assistant principal of my junior high school dropped menstrual blood on the floor of the store, which he proclaimed the formative moment in my aversion to vaginas. He talked about the possibility I perceived the vagina as a castrated male dripping blood, or as a device for castration—if I put my penis inside a vagina, it might not come out. I thought none of this but it didn't seem to matter. When I told him about my father's pornography collection hidden in a torn brown paper bag at the back of the top drawer of his dresser he scribbled furiously. When I told him how shocked I was to see Little Rich's penis, and how insecure it made me feel, he said that I shouldn't use Little Rich's penis as a reference.

I made no epiphanic connections with the perplexing Freudian explanations until one day, during one of my rambling, free-association monologues, I mentioned that when I was a toddler, before we moved above the store, we lived in a one-bedroom apartment in an ugly red brick apartment building on Foster Avenue. I didn't get my own bedroom until we moved to the apartment above the store when I was six years old.

At this Dr. Myers's presence changed, like a German shepherd catching the scent of a bitch in heat. "Where did you sleep before you got your own room?" he asked.

"I slept in the same room as my parents."

"In the same room for six years? How far away from your parents did you sleep?"

It was a small room, probably smaller than I even remembered. It was painted tan, like oatmeal mottled with a sponge, and the decorative moldings on the walls looked like empty picture frames. The dresser was too small for all our clothes and there were cardboard boxes of clothing stacked waist-high in the corners. I slept in a children's bed with a red vinyl headboard imprinted with a Japanese pagoda and a geisha standing by a stream, probably only four or five feet from my parents' bed.

"Four or five feet?" Dr. Myers asked. "And where did your parents have sex?"

I never thought about my parents having sex. "I don't know where they had sex," I said.

"They probably had sex only four or five feet away from you," he said. "About as close as you're sitting now to the door."

I glanced at the door to my room uncomfortably. "No, they wouldn't have," I said.

"How can you be so certain? In all those years you slept in the same room, don't you think your parents had intercourse?"

"Well, not in the same room as me," I said.

"But where then?" he persisted.

"Probably in the living room," I suggested. But then I remembered we had that peculiarly shaped arced sofa in the living room, like a slice of cantaloupe. They'd had to have been acrobats to have sex on that sofa. Where then? On the floor? I tried to picture my parents having sex on the floor of the living room with me asleep in the bedroom. "If they had sex in front of me, wouldn't I have remembered it?" I asked.

"Of course you wouldn't have remembered it," Dr. Myers said. "You were a child. You would've blocked it out. Watching your parents have intercourse would have been a terrifying experience for you. Depending on what you saw them doing, you could've thought your mother was being hurt by your father, or even killed. Groans of pleasure are very easily interpreted as pain by an infant. Oral sex can be seen as cannibalistic. An infant has no way to understand what the most important people in the world are doing to each other. It's extremely traumatizing."

"It never happened," I said.

"Think about it for a minute. If you slept in the same bedroom with your parents for six years—that's over two thousand nights—don't you think they had sex at least *once* while you were in your bed? The odds are they had intercourse in front of you many times."

"It never happened," I repeated.

"Look, if you could remember one time, just one incident, it would be a step in the right direction to under-standing your homosexuality."

But I refused to believe it, and I argued with him about it session after session, until, at an impasse, I was deter-mined to refute it.

The Contessa

"My darling Richard," said a young woman of noble bear-ing standing in the doorway of the card room. She posed there briefly, dressed in black slacks and gray cashmere sweater, her hands on her hips, looking as though she had been lolling about in a ski chalet in Gstaad instead of locked up in Payne Whitney. Before she said another word I had a crush on her. She was my first fag hag.

"Congratulations!" Mr. Halliday cheered. "It's about time they moved you down." He extended his arms and they embraced and kissed cheeks and patted each other on the back.

"The patients on six were either absolute nutters or brain dead from electroshock therapy," she said in an ac-cent that was neither French nor Italian nor British. "Not exactly stimulating conversationalists." She turned to me, smiling warmly, and she reminded me of Tina Mastriano. "And who is this?" she asked.

"This is my friend Steven who helps me with my jig-saw puzzles," Mr. Halliday said. "Steven, this is Alessan-dra, who was my only pal on the sixth floor."

"You're a little cutie," she said, taking me in. "How old are you?"

"Fifteen," I said shyly.

"Fifteen? Are you a virgin?"

I was too stunned to speak.

"You don't have to answer that," Mr. Halliday jumped in when he saw how flustered I was.

"No matter if you are or aren't," Alessandra continued, reaching out and tugging on the sleeve of my sweater. "Nothing to be embarrassed about. Or that can't be fixed. Where are you from?"

"Brooklyn."

"Brooklyn! The home of the Dodgers!" she said.

"And Coney Island," I added, trying to be interesting.

"I hear all the boys in Brooklyn have big cocks," she said offhandedly.

"You don't have to respond to that, either." Mr. Halliday said.

"It wasn't a question," Alessandra scolded.

I was shocked when she said all the boys had big cocks in Brooklyn, but it sounded really terrific with her sexy accent, which she told me was "mid-continent ennui." Alessandra's pastiche of an accent made everything she said sound charming, including "cunt," "suck," and "fuck," which she said often. She was a handful. She was twenty-five, the person closest in age to me on the floor. Her mother was a British glue heiress—whatever that meant, I never asked, I just acted impressed—and her late father was of obscure Italian nobility who made his money in cashmere in Piacenza, the cashmere capital of Italy. That officially made her Alessandra, the contessa de Piacenza.

"Are you sure?" I asked Mr. Halliday in confidence. "Is she a real contessa?"

"Oh yes," he said. "And notorious." Mr. Halliday knew

about her because when she was eighteen years old she caused a scandal in Great Britain by having an affair with a movie star thirty years her senior. She was photographed topless with him on the balcony of a hotel in Sitges, and the photo was published in all the tabloids. She wound up in Payne Whitney because on her way back to Paris from getting a nifty bias-cut hairdo at Sassoon in London, she was caught at Heathrow Airport with fifty bucks' worth of heroin in her purse, which she occasionally sniffed, she said, for fun. After her arrest, her drug dealer sold his story to the *Daily Mail* and she was tabloid fodder for another week. The tabloids quoted one of her French boyfriends as saying she was a nymphomaniac and sexually insatiable. She had a choice of either jail or a psychiatric hospital— there were no rehabs back then—and she opted for Payne Whitney.

Alessandra was pals with a certain sullen, darkly handsome actor with honey-brown eyes, who had been nominated for a supporting actor Oscar a few years before. Within days of meeting her I heard in detail what every single part of his body looked like, which she spoke of with unseemly delight. When she realized what a prude I was, she delighted in embarrassing me. One day she took my breath away by walking too close to me in a doorway, the back of her hand brushing the front of my pants. She did it again, a few days later, but it was so casual I could never be certain if it was intentional.

I developed another adolescent crush, this time on a melancholic woman in her thirties named Deedee Conklin, who made sadness seem chic. Even her depression was elegant; it lingered like her Joy perfume when she left a room. She was the art director of an architecture magazine, and although her bangs and wispy forelocks made her look French, she was a Boston Brahmin and spoke with a Beacon Hill accent. Deedee was delusional, the other patients decided, because she claimed she had been the girlfriend of the newly elected president, John F. Kennedy. Deedee said that the affair started back in Hyannis Port and went on for years, but when J.F.K. decided to run for president he cut off all contact with her. She took it pretty hard, swallowed too many pills, accidentally she said, and that's how she ended up in Payne Whitney. At the time nobody knew anything about Kennedy's relationship with Marilyn Monroe, nor the dozens of other women who had yet to come forward to say they were also his conquests, so we took Deedee's claim that she slept with the president with a grain of salt. It was a mental hospital after all, and if someone tells you they're Marie of Romania, you just say, "Sure."

At dinner one night Deedee suggested that instead of holding my knife and fork clenched in my fists like a caveman, I hold them in the European style. She showed me how to eat with the fork turned down and to cut my food with the knife in my right hand, and it immediately felt comfortable to me. Next she suggested that I put the knife and fork down on the plate while I was chewing. She also told me to take my napkin off the table, and to put my cotton hopsacking hip-huggers in the garbage. She said that well-dressed boys my age wore chinos. With cordovan penny loafers. From Brooks Brothers on Madison Avenue.

Not really knowing what chinos or cordovan penny loafers or Brooks Brothers was, I called my bewildered mother in Brooklyn and begged her to go to Brooks Brothers and buy chinos and loafers for me. A week later a new outfit was delivered at the front desk. Deedee made me check on the sole of the shoes to see if "Brooks Brothers" was stamped in the leather, just in front of the heel, to be sure they were the real deal.

All the other patients thought I looked spiffy in my new duds, and now Mr. Halliday suggested I get rid of my tortured pompadour. He said that while fashion was important, haircuts could be transformative. He explained that when he and Mother were in New Haven with *South Pacific*, Josh Logan didn't want Bill Tabbert as Lieutenant Cable, the second lead, because he didn't think he was sexy enough. Mr. Halliday and Mother cut and dyed Tabbert's hair in the hotel one night and the next day Josh Logan *didn't even recognize* Tabbert at rehearsals, and he became a big hit in the show. "It wasn't just a disguise," Halliday said. "It gave him confidence." So the next time the hospital barber came by our floor he gave me what would have amounted to a crew cut had my hair had not been so silky that it didn't stand up. Instead, it coated my head like the blond fuzz on a baby chick. The haircut peeled away a layer. Without all that carefully combed hair, my face was less childishly rounded, and there was a rakish cleft in my chin that had hardly been an indentation ten pounds before.

In the afternoons Alessandra came and sat with us. We watched the boats go by on the river as the setting sun turned Queens and Roosevelt Island into gold and orange landscapes. Alessandra told us about private school in Switzerland, and lesbian affairs she had, and Mr. Halliday told us stories about being on the road with *South Pacific* and how Mother suggested she actually wash her hair on-stage every night, but she regretted it because it dried her hair out. And once she cartwheeled off the stage right into the orchestra pit and nearly killed herself, so they cut the cartwheel, but I don't remember what show that was from. In May we started a new puzzle together, Botticelli's *Birth of Venus*, and I was the happiest I had been in a long time.

I felt like Eliza Doolittle at the psycho country club. I quietly appreciated that Payne Whitney was my chrysalis, and that I was evolving in unexpected ways. I began to think of it even more as a hotel, perhaps a cruise ship, afloat. Maybe it was a ship of crazies, but I had embarked on a voyage where almost anything was possible.

Peter Pan and the Lost Boy

Finally, Peter Pan was going to alight on the third floor.

On the day of her visit I wore a long-sleeve madras shirt and sat in a chair within sight of the front door, reading an old book that I got from the hospital library cart that came around once a week, *A Stone for Danny Fisher*, by Harold Robbins, my mother's favorite author. I read the book so intently while I waited for Peter Pan that the words blurred and my eyes began to ache. I had to pee but I dared not abandon my post. Finally the doorbell rang and a nurse came from the office to unlock the big oak door. Then there she was, Mother. My foolish heart, be still! She was wearing a scarf, tweed overcoat with a fur collar, and boots. I expected Mr. Halliday to come out of his room, sweep down the hallway, and cry, "Mother!" and Mary Martin to sigh, "Father!" and then sink into each other's arms. Instead, there was a demure peck on the cheek from Mr. Halliday, a coy look from Mother, a sly smile back from him, a lingering hug for both of them during which she put her head on his chest and closed her eyes. Sweet. I got the feeling it was the shy embrace of a couple making up after a long, bad argument. Arm in arm, they walked down the hall to his room without even glancing in my direction and shut the door behind them. He forgot to introduce me! I groaned aloud in frustration.

The nurse who had unlocked the door for Mother gave me a big smile, like, "Wasn't that exciting?"

No, it was only half-exciting because he didn't introduce me. The days leading up to Mary Martin's visit I fawned so on Mr. Halliday lest he forget his promise to introduce me that I can't imagine how he endured it. I rehearsed in my head the scene of my introduction hundreds of times—what she would say, what I would say, how she would take a shine to me and invite me to sit with them during her visit, and then Mr. Halliday would give me a role in his next Broadway show.

Determined to meet her, I stayed glued to my chair for the entire two hours of visiting time. It was agony. I was dying to pee but I couldn't give up my post. I plowed through *A Stone for Danny Fisher* until a chime rang signaling visiting time was up. Presently Mr. Halliday and Mother emerged from his room and walked down the hall toward the big oak door, holding hands. Finally he noticed me sitting there, looking like a starved dog, and beckoned me over. I bounded up to them and he introduced me to Mother as "a new acquaintance," which made me glow.

I stared at Mary Martin goofily. She was a middle-aged woman. Not a trace of Peter Pan. She had a pointy chin, a big nose for her little face, dark brown eyes, and the whitest teeth I had ever seen in a mouth. She smiled apprehensively, as if perhaps I might be an axe murderer, then she offered me her hand and said brightly, "It's so nice to meet you!" I was relieved to hear it was Peter Pan's voice when she spoke.

I made my toady speech about how thrilled I was to meet her, and that she was "greaaat" in *The Sound of Music*, and how I watched *Peter Pan* every time it was on TV. I nearly curtsied. She waited for me to say something more, but I had used up my prepared material so I just beamed at her.

"What is that you're reading?" she asked, pointing to the book I was holding. I held up my Harold Robbins paperback. "He's my mother's favorite author."

"He's very entertaining," she said politely.

"But that stuff is junk," Mr. Halliday sniffed. "It's not literature." He asked Mother, "What can we give my friend to read that's worth the paper it's printed on?"

Mother cocked her head and said, "You know what he should read? He should read *To Kill a Mockingbird*. Have you heard of that book?" she asked me.

I said I hadn't.

Mr. Halliday concurred that *To Kill a Mockingbird* would be a perfect book for me to read; it had won the Pulitzer Prize, and the movie of the book, starring Gregory Peck, was coming out next December. Mother said she'd drop off their copy of the book at the front desk later in the week. She wiggled her finger goodbye at me and I stumbled into my room in a daze. I sat in a chair, thrilled to my core, going over and over in my mind in slow motion the twenty seconds I was with her.

When *To Kill a Mockingbird* arrived I could hardly look up from its pages, pages that Saint Mary touched with her own hands. It wouldn't have mattered. I was enrapt from the first page. Reading it felt the way junkies must feel about heroin: there was no better sensation; nothing else mattered, except to get back to it. I fretted that I was reading it too fast, piggy in my pleasure, so I tried to allot myself only twenty pages a day, but it was hopeless, and I gulped it down in four or five sittings. I sobbed when I finished, to have to leave the people and world that Harper Lee had created, and I reluctantly returned the book to Mr. Halliday.

We talked about it for days. He was great to talk with about books. His years as a film critic and story editor in Hollywood had given him a keen sense of character development and storytelling. He said that the author, Harper Lee, was Scout, the tomboy. He asked me who I thought was the book's real hero, Atticus Finch or Boo Radley? He asked if I found it satisfying that Boo saves the children from the real villain. What about Dill, the character based on Truman Capote? Couldn't I just see how that boy would grow up to be Truman Capote?

Capote who?

A week later *Breakfast at Tiffany's* arrived at the front desk. I knew all about the movie because I had seen it at the Culver Theater, and I loved Audrey Hepburn's madcap version of Holly Golightly, for which she was nominated for an Academy Award. But Holly Golightly in the novella Truman Capote wrote was more like a hooker, and I hated the ambiguous ending, that she might have ended up in Africa somewhere. I slogged through it, though, and Mr. Halliday was a bit annoyed when I admitted I didn't like it. He explained why sometimes a movie needs to be different from the book, and that I could like them both on their own merits, so I changed my tune and pretended I liked the book much more on second thought. I should have kept my mouth shut, because he ordered up another Capote book for me to read—*Other Voices, Other Rooms*, a swampy, melancholy novel about a lost twelve-year-old in a strange household in Alabama. Mr. Halliday said the book was about self-acceptance being part of growing up, and I should take its message to heart.

And so it went. Every week a new book arrived, some of which I only politely pretended to like; others, like Carson McCullers's *The Member of the Wedding*, made me ache with the beauty of its writing. "How does Carson McCullers *do* that?" I asked myself every few pages, parsing the words in each sentence, trying to figure out how she was able to take me into that kitchen in Georgia, inside Frankie's head, and imbue in me all the shadows and sounds and smells of her world. Mr. Halliday said that although you can learn to write, what Carson McCullers does is genius, which can't be learned, and that another genius was the actress Julie Harris—a friend of his and Mother's from the theater world—who had captured Frankie right off the pages of the book in the play and the movie, and was nominated for an Oscar for the movie version, which came out when I was only six years old, too young to see it at the Culver.

"You'll be interested to know that Carson McCullers was a graduate of Payne Whitney University," Mr. Halliday said.

"Not really!"

"Oh yes, she was right here, probably on this floor. Maybe she slept in your bed."

Maybe she did. They sure hadn't replaced the mattresses since McCullers signed herself in after a suicide attempt in 1948. As I would discover, Payne Whitney had impressive alumni, including notable writers and members of the arts, probably thousands over its history. Not unexpectedly, William S. Burroughs spent time there in 1940 after cutting off his finger, despondent over the infidelities of his lover. Jean Stafford, the Pulitzer Prize–winning novelist and short-story writer, was a Payne Whitney patient two weeks short of a year in 1946–47, treated for depression and alcoholism. She had nicknamed the tiny park in which we walked every day "Luna Park." While she was hospitalized Stafford wrote to a friend describing "a most gruesome dance in the gymnasium where all the crazy men met up with all the crazy women and danced to the music of a sedate four piece orchestra. Some of the ladies' husbands came and it did seem sad and most touchingly sincere." She continued writing from the hospital, and the doctors gave her an afternoon pass to have her author's photo taken at the Central Park Zoo for *The Mountain Lion*. Publisher Robert Giroux was on her approved visitors' list. In 1954 her husband, the Pulitzer Prize–winning poet Robert Lowell, signed himself into PWC (a "thorough and solid place," he called it), where he was diagnosed as manic-depressive and given shock treatment. In 1975 novelist Mary McCarthy would re-create a stay in the hospital in her book *The Group*, when one of her characters is tricked into signing herself into the hospital by a scheming husband. In the 1970s the New York poet James Schuyler wrote several poems while in residence titled, "The Payne Whitney Poems."

The last book Mr. Halliday gave me to read was a bestseller of the moment, *Youngblood Hawke*, a novel by

Herman Wouk, whose work I knew from the movie of his novel, *Marjorie Morningstar. Hawke* was about a writer from Kentucky who comes to New York to publish his first book; it was set in the glamorous and romantic world of New York publishing, of editors and agents and smart dinner parties, and when Hawke writes a bestseller he buys a townhouse on West 11th Street, which turned out to be as prophetic as you can get.

In April thousands of tulips planted along the driveways and paths of the New York Hospital campus all came into bloom the same week, and there was a spectacular display of colors below my windows, a few warm days and a promise of renewal, and New York and I began to shake off the winter and slide into spring.

Music Soothes the Savage Breast

Although I talked to my mom and dad on the phone an allotted ten minutes, three times a week, from a claustrophobic phone booth near the nurses' station that reeked of chain-smoked cigarettes, I hadn't seen them in over two months. When they walked through the big oak door on the third floor for the first time, I could see by the look on their faces they were surprised to find a sleeker, metropolitan version of me. I was stunned to see their shellacked provincialism.

I was a traitorous piece of shit. If I was in a Fanny Hurst novel I would have denied them and pretended they were there to see another patient, as in the movie *Imitation of Life*, when light-skinned Susan Kohner, who was nominated for an Oscar, runs away from home to be a showgirl in Las Vegas, and pretends Juanita Moore (who was also nominated) isn't her mother when she comes to find her backstage because she's a "Negro." I was mortified by my mother's blue-black dyed hair, teased into a beehive with a wave-like shape coming out of the right side of her head, by her two-piece wool suit and big pocketbook, her costume jewelry with beads the size of lightbulbs, and my dad's glen plaid sport jacket from Wallachs that fit him as though he had left the hanger in it.

We retired to my room, where for the next hour I boorishly lectured them about Mary Martin, table manners, bad*minton* (not *mitten*), and delirium tremens. My mother, although perplexed, tried to be excited for my new sophistication and mental patient friends, but my father was threatened by what it all meant, and he got pricklier by the moment.

The gossip from 18th Avenue didn't travel well. What might have enthralled me a few months ago paled against Deedee Conklin's revelation about sleeping with John F. Kennedy. Gog didn't come home one night and my grandmother and Katherine had to take the Long Island Rail Road to Freeport and the taxi from the train station to the house cost five dollars. My father got into an argument with the assistant principal of his school, who shook his fist at him, and my dad lodged a formal complaint with the Board of Education, another in a long trail of incidents that precipitated my dad's transfer to a new school every few years. The rest of the news—the saleswomen, the store, the Culver Luncheonette—were all caught in stop-action from months ago. When I returned they would be in exactly the same place I had left them.

Meantime, my train had left the station. I realized that

part of me didn't ever want to go back to 18th Avenue. I wanted to be with the other patients in Payne Whitney. I belonged with them. I knew the other patients were eccentric, or crazy, but they were also accomplished and smart, and deliciously complicated, and I wanted to live in their world, for better or worse. So I decided to wade into troubled waters to get there.

"Dad, there are some things I talked about with the doctor that I need to ask you," I said.

"Anything I can do to help," he pledged gallantly.

"Remember you told me that your mother jumped from roof to roof so she could follow you to school, to make sure you were safe? How could momma jump from roof to roof?"

"I never said that," he answered, looking surprised. "I told you that when I was a little boy she went up to the roof of the building where we lived and she watched me until I crossed the street safely."

Surely he had told me about her jumping from roof to roof. "That's funny," I said. "I could have sworn . . ."

"No such thing ever happened," he interrupted. "I don't know where you got that from."

I shrugged. I supposed I could have made up the part about her jumping from roof to roof. "Do you remember rehearsing me about what to do if somebody stopped me on the street and told me to get into their car?" I asked.

"What, am I on trial?"

"No, no. But you said you were going to help. I need to know this for my analysis. Did you think I was going to get kidnapped?"

"Parents talk to their children about kidnappers," my mother said.

"But we weren't rich," I said. "Why would I be kidnapped?"

My father looked grim. "There are people who take children for reasons other than money," he said.

Ah. They were afraid I was going to be molested, not kidnapped. "Is that why you forbid me to use the bathroom at the Culver Theater?"

"Who knew who went up there?" my mother said. "You were a little boy alone in the movie theater. It was just as easy for you to come down the street and use the bathroom in the store."

It sounded so reasonable now.

"Is that why you didn't let me stay in the school yard after school? You were afraid that I'd get molested?"

My father snorted. "You could've stayed in the school yard," he said. "You didn't *want* to be in the school yard. You wanted to be in the store. In a box."

"But you told me that you didn't want me to go to the school yard because when you were a little boy you were kicked by another kid in the school yard. You had a rupture, and they fixed it with muscles from a lamb."

"Where do all these stories come from?" he asked, shaking his head. He began to do that thing with his eyebrows going up and down when he was angry. "I was kicked when I was six years old," he conceded, "but nobody ever said anything about an operation or a lamb."

He was lying. I remembered him telling me about the operation. Or did I? I felt like Ingrid Bergman in *Gaslight*, for which she won the Oscar for best actress: her husband, the wonderful Charles Boyer, tries to drive her insane by playing tricks on her, including turning the gaslight up and down, up and down. Could I have been wrong about *all* these things I thought my father told me? If none of it was true, then Dr. Myers's analysis and interpretations were a Freudian house of cards.

So I waded in further. "There's something else I wanted to ask," I said.

My father gave me an "I dare you!" look.

"It's hard to ask," I said. "I need to know . . . when we lived on Foster Avenue . . . and we all slept in the same bedroom . . . where did you have sex?"

"I beg your pardon?" Now his eyebrows sprang up like a dog's hackles.

"Where did you and Mom have sex?" I repeated. I looked toward my mother for help, but she only shook her head in wonder. "When we lived on Foster Avenue, and we all slept in the same room, where did you have sex?"

"Stevie, Stevie," my mother implored. "Please don't."

"But I *need* to know," I insisted. "You've got to understand, I need to know this for my analysis."

"Is this the kind of crap the doctor is asking you?" my father demanded, his eyebrows now signaling an impending eruption. I was wondering how big an eruption he would dare to have in the hospital, lest they put *him* in the Quiet Room.

"I was rambling on in session one day," I explained. "It's called 'free association.' Whatever comes to your mind. It's Freud." I looked to my father for recognition. "He's a psychiatrist from Vienna—"

"*I know who Freud is!*" my father bellowed. "It's all about *sex*." He glared at me so hard when he said "sex" that his head trembled. "My personal life with your mother is none of your business," he went on, red and blustery. "And if this is the kind of crap that the doctor is feeding you, I'll pull you right out of here, mister."

"If you didn't have sex in front of me just say so," I challenged him.

"I don't have to say *anything!*" he said, standing up and putting on his coat. "Let's go, Ruthie," he ordered my mother.

My mother remained seated. "Why *this*?" she asked. "What's the point of this?"

"The doctor said it might matter," I told her.

"Ruthie, I said *let's go!*" my father demanded.

I held my mother's gaze like he wasn't even in the room. It was telepathy; I needed to know the truth and she needed to tell me.

"Yes," she said. "Sometimes we made love while you were asleep."

"*You must stop this!*" my father erupted, trying to lift her by her arm, but she resisted being pulled up. "*Ruthie, let's go!*" he pleaded, in a panic now.

I was stupefied. "While I was *asleep?*"

"We turned on the radio so you wouldn't hear," she said. "We played music sometimes next to your bed."

"You played *music?*" I asked, mystified that they could think that the radio would be some sort of screen. "How many times did this happen?"

"I don't know," she said, starting to cry.

"Ten times?" I asked her. "A *hundred* times?"

"*As many times as we wanted!*" my father shouted. He was trembling with rage and I thought he might cry too.

A nurse appeared at the door. "Is everything all right?" she asked.

"No, it is not all right," my father said.

"Then perhaps visiting time is over and you should leave," the nurse suggested.

I ignored her. "And I never woke up?" I begged my mother. "All the times you were just a few feet away in the next bed, I never woke up?"

"Once," my mother said, standing up, fumbling with her coat. "You woke up once. You were in your crib, maybe three years old, and I realized you had pulled yourself up and you were standing and shaking the side of the crib and crying."

I woke up. I saw them.

"I'm sorry," my mother said. "We didn't mean to do anything that would hurt you."

"Ruthie, I'm leaving without you," my father threatened, bolting out the door.

"We didn't know any better," my mother said. "But the Puerto Ricans all sleep ten in a room and it doesn't hurt them." Then she went down the hall after him, and the nurse followed to let them out.

Dr. Myers said it didn't matter if my father denied the things about his mother jumping over rooftops or having lamb tendons put in his groin. What mattered more was that they were my beliefs, they were totems, and if they weren't true, why I made up those specific things was just as important. But what mattered most, he said, was that I *had* seen them have sex, and I had been an unwilling partner in a forbidden ménage à trois. It was possible that it made me homosexual, and I had made a giant step confirming it. Now the real work in curing me could proceed.

Small Slam

"Who fucking did this?"

I could hear Mr. Halliday shouting from all the way down the hall. He had just gone into the sunroom and found an empty card table. His puzzle had vanished. He stomped down the hall to the nurses' office, where he was told to calm down. He was informed that his doctor had ordered the puzzle confiscated because the puzzle was interfering with his therapy. He was focusing too much attention on it, using it as a distraction to avoid dealing with his problems.

I knew immediately that they were wrong. The puzzle kept him sane, and it *was* therapeutic, because all the time he was fitting jigsaw pieces together he was certainly thinking, thinking, thinking about his life.

Halliday was beside himself. He cursed and paced and called his doctor a "cocksucker," and went back to his room to sulk.

Later that morning, gossip had it that Harold Kellogg had instigated the confiscation by complaining to the nurses that Mr. Halliday and his puzzle had appropriated the card table in the sunroom. When Halliday heard this he marched over to Kellogg's room to confront him. The door was open and Mr. Halliday stood in the threshold and glowered at him so fiercely that it was no wonder bolts of lightning didn't come out of his eyes. Kellogg glared right back, his bushy white eyebrows standing out like the quills on a porcupine.

Mr. Halliday wasn't without a diversion for long. Soon after his puzzle was confiscated, Mother dropped off a square piece of canvas mesh from a fancy needlepoint shop on Lexington Avenue with three fat avocados air-brushed on it, and Mr. Halliday began to needlepoint a throw-pillow cover. He needlepointed as much as he had worked on the jigsaw puzzle. It was just as mindlessly hypnotic—even more mindless—so I don't know what the nurses and doctors thought they'd accomplished.

"Come on," he said with a resigned sigh, when he saw me longingly watching him doing his needlepoint in the lounge. "Pull up a chair and I'll show you how to do it." He pulled a single strand of soft green yarn from a tangle of wool, threaded his needle, and began to stitch on the mesh, just the right tension, not too tight or loose or all the stitches wouldn't match, an exacting repetition that was soothing to watch. Mr. Halliday said that he and Mother loved to needlepoint, and that their Manhattan apartment was full of pillows. He said that when he got out of the hospital he was going to put this particular pillow in their house in South America, where they were going to retire. He talked to me wistfully about Buenos Aires and how beautiful and calm it was, and how soon they would spend all of their time on the farm, with Broadway far away.

I hoped Mr. Halliday appreciated that I didn't abandon him because the puzzle was gone, but without the puzzle there was nothing for me to do except listen. I decided that I should learn to needlepoint, so we could sit together and stitch and chat. I called home and asked them to send me a canvas and yarn, thinking I would surprise Mr. Halliday. My mother and father were again mystified, but they soldiered on and sent me a needle-point canvas of strawberries and brightly colored pink and red yarn.

I expected Mr. Halliday to be flattered when he discovered me sitting in a chair next to his with my own needlepoint, but he was aghast. "What do you think you're *doing*?" he gagged. He said that if I continued to do the needlepoint he would stop talking to me forever. I was so scared I hid it in my bottom drawer. I couldn't understand what I had done wrong. After that he was distant from me. I guessed my fawning embarrassed him.

Harold Kellogg had taken over the sunroom with his bridge game, which he played as obsessively as Mr. Halliday worked on his jigsaw puzzle. With Mr. Kellogg now presiding over the lounge, it turned very formal in that room. Mr. Halliday's favorite album, *Peter, Paul and Mary*, was turned off, the café conversation about theater and books was shut down, the most frequent words spoken were contract-bridge bids, and everybody called each other "partner" instead of their names. One afternoon I was hanging out in the lounge reading a magazine when I heard Mr. Kellogg at the card table complaining that there had been some sort of rift with a regular player and they were short a fourth. There was quiet discussion followed by muffled laughter and Kellogg said, "Any port in a storm." Then he called to me in his patrician voice, "Do you, by any chance, know how to play bridge?"

"Is bridge like canasta?" I asked hopefully.

There was more muffled laughter and further discussion, and then Kellogg asked, "Well, young man, would you fucking like to learn *how* to play bridge?"

I was thrilled to be asked, yet even more terrified. I took my place at the table opposite a former stockbroker who had endured two cycles of shock therapy that wiped out his knowledge of the stock market, to his dismay, yet his mind was sharp and clear when it came to cards. He didn't look up at me once that entire afternoon and hardly said a word except to bid.

"Now pay attention!" Kellogg ordered me. "What makes bridge so civilized is that it is only partially a game of intelligence and skill. It's also a game of rules and conventions in which people who enjoy playing bridge take pleasure." He rattled off a canon of incomprehensible rules, but I refused to give him the satisfaction of asking him to repeat anything, so I just nodded and murmured fake "ahh"s like I understood. Of course I was a risible player, but I was good at remembering what cards had been played. I played for two hours with them that afternoon, slowly getting more adept, soaking all of it in, even playing out a hand of three hearts and winning my bid, cheered on by the others. At the end of the rubber Mr. Kellogg practically had to force out the words, "Well done, neophyte."

The next day Mr. Kellogg made up with the regular fourth player and I was no longer needed. It hurt only a little. I never expected to become a regular. What mattered was that Harold Kellogg got to see that I was smart, and I earned his respect. After that he was civil enough to say hello to me when he passed me in the hall. It was as therapeutic as almost anything that happened at Payne Whitney.

A bad thing came out of it too. While I was engrossed in playing bridge that day, Mr. Halliday came down to the lounge and saw me playing with them. He was already annoyed with me about the copycat needlepoint, and he perceived my bridge game with Kellogg as a serious betrayal. From then on Mr. Halliday looked right through me, like Lily Williams used to do. "What's wrong?" I begged him.

"Why, nothing is wrong," he said airily.

I was sick at heart over it. Everybody on the floor noticed that he cut me off. One morning Miss Moneybags sneered at me in the dining room, "You boys break up?"

Six

Dog Days

That summer Payne Whitney was like a furnace. There was no air conditioning and the casement windows opened only halfway so nobody could jump out. I was moved up to the fourth floor and assigned a corner room with my own bath and a 1930s claw-footed tub, in which I took lukewarm bubble baths to cool off. When I lay in bed at night the leaves on the trees below my window rustled in the breezes coming off the East River, and I dreamed Payne Whitney would always be my home, and that I would live forever above the FDR Drive with the rich and neurasthenic.

Marilyn Monroe died early that August and her death hung over us, as oppressive as the heat. The whole nation was in shock, but inside Payne Whitney we were in emotional turmoil. There was a sense of despair among the patients, and two copycat suicides were attempted in the days after her death. It was all anybody could talk about. Did she overdose or was it an accident? We understood Monroe was in Payne Whitney for only a few days, but nevertheless she was ours. How could any of us ever be happy, if she had all that fame and money, and she killed herself? A little over a year before, she had signed herself out of the seventh floor and now she was dead. Some people said that if she had stayed she wouldn't be dead now; others said it was inevitable, people like her were doomed. We each quietly worried about what would happen to us when we got out, with our own potential suicides to contemplate.

Four was a big floor, twenty-four patients, a transitional unit from which people incrementally returned to the outside world—like dipping your toe into the reality pool before you took the plunge. The first dip was "walk privileges," daily promenades around the neighborhood. Some of the patients hadn't been outside the building in five or six months except for walks in the garden. Every afternoon at 4 p.m. groups of us would emerge from the doors of the psychiatric clinic looking like a Gahan Wilson cartoon, squinting in the sunlight, and set out on a meandering stroll through the local streets. Not everybody on the floor had walk privileges, assigned according to what kind of escape risk you were. If they let you outside, your doctor needed to believe with some certainty that you were going to return. There were cardinal rules about these walks. Patients had to stay with their prearranged group and not go off alone. We could wander only as far as we could walk—no taxis or car rides were permitted. It was forbidden to return to your home, even if it was just around the corner from the hospital. A patient could go into a store, if the group came with you, to purchase toiletries permitted in the hospital, but not prescription drugs or razor blades. The group had to be back on the fourth floor by the sixty-minute mark. If you broke any of the rules you turned not into a pumpkin but into a patient with no walk privileges, perhaps even a patient who was moved to another floor, or worse, not a patient at all, but discharged, banished.

More often than not a few of the groups would end up in the same coffee shop, called the Poacher's Den, on the corner of East 68th Street and First Avenue, where we crowded into adjoining booths and drank coffee and chain-smoked cigarettes, trading gossip about other patients and nurses and doctors. Within a few weeks I knew every-body's history, family traumas, suicide attempts, drug ad-dictions, and alcohol problems. There were inside jokes about what the other customers would think if they knew this motley crew of characters was on a stroll from the local asylum. There was an easy sense of camaraderie in our shared nuttiness, and those lighthearted moments in the coffee shop made me feel less ashamed that I had wound up in a psychiatric clinic.

As the walk groups got more adventuresome we dis-covered that if we walked fast enough we could reach the edge of Central Park by the thirty-minute mark for a quick fix of trees and grass. After months of being cooped up in the stolid limestone fortress, just to look at the beauty of Central Park for two minutes and suck up the verdant en-ergy it gave off was soul restoring. Then we made a U-turn and scurried back to the hospital like mice.

It was Mr. Kellogg who intimidated a walk group into breaking the rules, with some help from a gorgeous blue-sky afternoon. It startled me that the straitlaced Mr. Kel-logg was the first to break the rules, but I suppose it was that kind of blustery impatience with life that made him who he was. One Sunday he bullied me, Ellen the editor, and Agnes Charant, a pleasant but stiff Radcliffe grad whose family owned a newspaper in Montreal, into taking a Yellow cab ride through Central Park, and then to the Plaza hotel so he could have a "proper tea." His treat. All of it was a capital offense, and we were taking an awful chance, but Mr. Kellogg seemed to have such a craving for tea at the Plaza that we took an oath of secrecy and went along.

Kellogg was wearing a baby-blue seersucker suit, and a straw skimmer with Harvard's colors on the hat band. He hailed a Checker on the corner of East 68th Street and I sat on the jump seat while we toured through the park drive, the taxi windows open and the warm air blowing in my face. That ride through Central Park was like a cupid's arrow. It was a vivid moment, the first time I'd ever been on the winding, elegant drive, with the castle-like turrets of Central Park West towering over the park's edges. It was like being inside the drawings of a storybook. I had seen Central Park in many movies, but now, with a famous architect and the daughter of a publisher and an editor of books, I was *in* it, on my way to the Plaza hotel, where Eloise lived.

My infatuation with Manhattan grew even more intense when the cab pulled up in front of the hotel. The chaos itself was glamorous: mobs of dapper people in the street, a tangle of cars and limousines and taxis, and calliope music playing next to the Pulitzer fountain, where a semicircle of black hansom cabs was lined up, drawn by huge horses, impatiently pawing at the asphalt.

Kellogg led the way up the red carpet on the front steps of the hotel and through the gilded lobby to the marble-floored Palm Court, where we followed him like courtiers. He informed the maître d' in a clipped New England accent that we wanted tea and we were on a tight schedule. In a few moments we were seated at a table with white linen and a spray of pink roses in a tiny vase. On the other side of the room a string quartet was playing a waltz, and Mr. Kellogg hummed along. When our tea was slow to arrive, he lost his temper. "How long does it take to heat water?" he demanded of the poor waiter, and he was mean to the maître d' who came to the table to offer apologies. They brought out a scrumptious display of cakes and jams, with whipped cream in a big silver bowl. I wanted to taste every one of them, but I wasn't sure what to do so I mimicked the rest of our group, daintily drinking tea and munching on a scone. Mr. Kellogg paid the check and we raced outside, jumped into a cab, and made it back to the hospital exactly at our curfew. I was so thrilled with the experience that I must have thanked Mr. Kellogg ten times until he told me, "Enough already."

Kellogg was discharged a month later. The staff and patients threw him a little party in the dining room and served chocolate donuts and milk. Mr. Halliday didn't attend. Harold Field Kellogg, I read in the *New York Times* in 1990, died at the age of seventy-two, of coronary disease, on the island of Nantucket, where he had retired.

Patients on the fourth floor also were given weekend passes to visit home, but I wasn't allowed to go to Brooklyn yet, lest I be exposed to the full blast of everything that waited for me on 18th Avenue. On weekends the fourth floor was mostly empty, and a little lonely. Maybe it was the inescapable heat one Saturday in August, but I was horny all day. I had nonstop sexual fantasies, and I wanted desperately to go to my room and masturbate, but with so little activity on the floor it was easy to get caught by a nurse, and I had pledged to Dr. Myers that I would not masturbate and fantasize about boys.

In a heat-induced trance, I walked down to the south lounge hoping to catch a breeze off the East River. The lounge was empty so I found an *Esquire* magazine and sat down in a chair and thumbed through it until I found a men's underwear ad in the back. I sat and stared at it for a moment, and then I rubbed the magazine against my erection through my pants, and just like that, uncontrollably, I had an orgasm. I gasped and shook a little in the chair, and then lazily opened my eyes from my post-orgasmic coma to see Alessandra curled up on the sofa on far side of the room watching me. She had been there all along, so still that I hadn't seen her. Now she stretched and yawned like a cat waking up. I held my breath until she said something, which was, "A great American writer."

"Huh?" I managed to say, miserable and all sticky in my pants. I wanted the floor to open up and swallow me.

She held up the book she had been reading, *Day of the Locust.* "Nathanael West," she said. "Hollywood and desperation. Meaningless lives. Sound familiar?"

"I didn't see you sitting there," I said.

"I gathered," she answered smoothly. "Don't worry, I have two brothers. I'm used to catching fifteen-year-old boys having a wank."

"I was not!" I protested. I stormed out of the room, in an odd crouch, hiding the front of my pants with the magazine. I looked ridiculous and it was all she could do not to laugh.

Alessandra discreetly never made reference to the incident, but I could never look her in the eye without thinking about it. Perhaps the most disturbing aspect of this story was that she walked away from the clinic a few weeks later and I never saw her again. She lingered behind one day after occupational therapy—she hid, I guess—and took an elevator down with visitors and strolled home. She was such a free spirit, I'm sure being locked up was soul killing for her. I read about her in the society columns for years after that. She cleaned up her act, got married to a rich guy in the movie business, and moved to Beverly Hills. I sometimes think I should call her up and say hello, but I'm sure she'd hate that.

Moon Over Miami

I had a little less than three weeks left before my grandfather's money ran out and my stay at Payne Whitney was over, and nothing seemed resolved. Wasn't the promise that once I understood my problems I would feel better? I did feel better, but that was because I was having such a good time at Payne Whitney. But I began to worry there would be no resolution before my grandfather's gift ran out and it was time for me to go home.

Weeks passed in therapy uneventfully while Dr. Myers interpreted my dreams. His interpretations sometimes seemed arbitrary and convenient. In a dream, according to him, my mother could be represented by my father, or a misty character was really him, Dr. Myers. Or a dream about being scared on the Steeplechase in Coney Island when I was a kid was actually about having an erection. Then there were all the dream fragments about Miami Beach, dozens of them. Miami Beach things popped up in my dreams all the time; even when the dream happened somewhere else, there was a piece of Miami Beach in them, the white front steps of the National Hotel, the nighttime miniature golf across from Pickin' Chicken, the tiny paper parasols stuck in the strawberry shortcake.

It was odd that I dreamed about it so often, because I had only been to Miami Beach once, I told Dr. Myers, when I was seven years old, but it was still very fresh to me. It was March, and Gog had surprised us with a gift of three round-trip plane tickets for my mom and dad and me, plus a week at the National Hotel on Collins Avenue, right on the ocean. We were flying on a Douglas DC 4, the fastest plane in the sky, and it would take only four and a half hours to get to Florida. Gog gave my mom and me the tickets in the store one afternoon, and I was so thrilled that I danced up and down the length of the store while Katherine sang "Moon Over Miami," and everybody clapped.

But when my dad got home from work that evening he was in a grouchy mood because he had a fight with somebody at his father's seltzer bottling plant, Jacob Goldberg & Sons, where he worked at the time. Jake Goldberg, *Poppy Alta*, was a peasant from Poland with a crazy, junkyard smile—one tooth, half-a-tooth, no tooth, a gold crown. My dad claimed *Alta* could bite an eighth-inch-thick piece of glass with those teeth and spit out the chunks. His wife, Leah, was a tough old bird with crepe-paper skin and two red cauliflower blooms of high blood pressure on her cheeks. She relaxed by playing solitaire at the kitchen table in the finished basement, chewing sunflower seeds, spitting the husks into her fist like a machine gun. She smoked, a pack of unfiltered Camel cigarettes a day, and every few minutes she exploded in a cascading smoker's cough until she was red-faced and doubled over. Leah was wary of me. Even as a child I could see by the way she gazed at me that she knew I was a *rara avis* and not part of her durable tribe. She died of a cerebral hemorrhage at age eighty one summer night while playing canasta at the Six Lake House bungalow colony in the Catskills. The other players said she closed her eyes, passed gas, and slid to the floor.

When my mother put dinner on the table, she cautiously told my dad about the trip. She said that Gog thought we all needed a break—my dad worked so hard—and he had bought us plane tickets and a week's stay at the National Hotel, and did my dad think his father would give him a week off at work?

No, he said, it was out of the question. They lived paycheck to paycheck and Miami Beach was expensive. Where would the money come from for meals and tips and all the other expenses? He said that Gog was intruding in our lives and instigating family fights. Sure, Gog could take off a week to go see his whores in Miami Beach, but not people like my dad, who worked hard for a living, carrying cartons of seltzer bottles up and down six flights of steps ten hours a day. He told my mother to give back the plane tickets.

I kneeled next to him, and took his hand and pleaded, but he was resolute—we were not going. I went to bed sobbing and I could hear my mother crying on the kitchen phone with Gog. Later that night, Katherine, the *vermittler*, stopped by our apartment to talk to my dad on her way home from a bingo game at Holy Ghost church. I don't know what sorcery she used, but in the morning my dad relented and said we could go, as long as he could get the week off. I was so grateful I grabbed on to him and he lifted me up into his arms and I kissed his neck with gratitude.

The day of departure he was thin-lipped and scowling, getting tense over things like the zipper not closing on the garment bag. We were on the way to Idlewild Airport, my mother and I in a euphoric mood, when she said something funny and she and I laughed—I don't know what she said, and it doesn't matter—I just remember her laughing like a young girl, with her head back, she looked beautiful, we were both so merry. And then he snapped, his fury sudden and shocking. I guess his anger had been on the boil since he grudgingly changed his mind about going. He began to turn the steering wheel erratically to the right and left, as though he were struggling with an unseen hand trying to drive us off the road and crash the car. My mom grabbed on to the dashboard, pleading, "Izzy, Izzy, slow down! I didn't mean anything!"

He steered us all over the Belt Parkway, raging against Gog and his "who-ers," and against my mother, a "fat cow," and he said he was sick of me, that I embarrassed him in front of Irving the Jeweler last week by demanding to go home for dinner when he was talking politics.

"I didn't do anything!" I shouted at him. "You pick on us! I hate you!"

With that, he reached inside the pocket of his tweed overcoat and took out the navy blue Eastern Airlines ticket folders, ripped them in half, and threw them out the window. For a second one of the folders caught on the inside edge of the window frame before it fluttered away down the parkway, cars running over it.

"What did I *do*?" my mother begged him, sobbing. She

began to beat herself hard on the head and face with her fist. I was terrified. "What did I *do*?" she howled.

I tried to grab her wrists from the backseat to stop her from hitting herself, but it was no use. I felt so sorry for her, for me, for our lives. I looked around in the backseat of the car for something to stab my father in the neck with—a screwdriver, a pencil—but there was nothing, and I collapsed in a heap on the floor of the car and sobbed. My father got off the parkway at the next exit and turned around, driving us home in threatening silence. He pulled over once in Sheepshead Bay for me to throw up by the curb.

My father stopped talking to all of us and we lived with our heads down, in mourning. I saw those plane tickets fluttering down the Belt Parkway a thousand times in my mind. Still see them now.

I told Dr. Myers about a cold morning two weeks later, when my mother woke me before dawn, just after my father left for work on his seltzer delivery route. My eyes were closed but I could smell my grandmother's Jean Naté perfume, clean and sweet, and when I opened my eyes she was there too, in her mink coat, her honey-blond hair teased and sprayed, and she called me her "little man." Gog was there also, wearing an overcoat and muffler, and he was laughing.

It was hard to wake up a seven-year-old from a deep sleep, so they pulled on my socks and pants while I was still drowsy. I had to wake up, they said, because we had plane tickets for the first flight out from Idlewild, and we only had five minutes to pack. My mother jumped in the shower, threw a few things in a bag, and we were out the door, her hair still wet. I was half asleep as Gog carried me in his arms out to his Cadillac with the pointy tail fins, and drove us away from 18th Avenue. Arthur Godfrey was on the car radio, and my grandmother said that Arthur Godfrey owned a restricted hotel in Miami Beach called the Kenilworth and that we would never go there. My mother tried to comb the tangles out of her wet hair but her comb broke and she was upset until Gog said there were combs in Miami Beach, and we all laughed at how silly it was, and no one got mad at our laughter. My grandmother held my hand tightly so I wouldn't get lost while we rushed through the Eastern Airlines terminal to the boarding gate and out onto the tarmac where the plane sat waiting, mammoth and breathtaking. I had a window seat, and there were giant propellers right outside the window, and they were loud and scary. We went up and down in the sky over the ocean, like a loop-de-loop.

When the plane landed at Miami Airport Gog held my hand as we stepped out onto a platform at the top of a flight of metal stairs and the warm, damp air caressed me, so soft and sultry it made me euphoric and slightly dizzy. That very afternoon I was bobbing up and down in the waves with Gog, the ocean a watercolor wash of aquamarines and emeralds, as warm as a bathtub. High tide had left the pebbly beach littered with Portuguese men-of-war, like hundreds of pink chewing gum bubbles along the shore. They had long, lacy tentacles that caused a painful blister, and Gog and I went up and down the beach and popped them with shovels. We ate lunch at a table by the pool while I dried in the sun wearing my new swim trunks and matching terry cloth–lined top. "It's a cabana set," I told a woman in the elevator, going up to our room. On Saturday night we went to the hotel nightclub, my face glowing with suntan, and the comedian who talked to me from the stage asked if I bet on the horses. The audience laughed, and he bought me a Coke.

Everybody was laughing in Miami Beach. It was a city in celebration, it seemed. It felt happy, it looked happy; the buildings were low and white stucco, curved and not sharp, and the sky was everywhere, no end to it. Every night after dinner we strolled the promenade of Lincoln Road, a hundred feet wide, pieces of the moonlight glittering in the coral rock pavement. Everyone was deeply tanned, men wore sports jackets and women wore mink stoles, no matter how warm it was, and we window-shopped at Saks Fifth Avenue and Peck & Peck. My mom and I had a room overlooking the ocean and we slept to the sound of the surf in a big bed with crisp white sheets and pillowcases. My sunburn felt good on the fresh-laundered sheets, and I had my mother all to myself, my father's dolor back in Brooklyn except for occasional phone calls from home, his voice crackling from the receiver like an electrical current, and the *click* when he hung up on my mother.

The dream ended. Our time was up. We had to go home. I arrived at Idlewild Airport with a stuffed alligator and a coconut under my arm, mementos of irreplaceable times. We returned to find trouble. While we were away my father hadn't shown up for work one day. Alta had fired him and they stopped speaking. My dad's excuse was that he went to the Culver movie theater and fell asleep in the smoking section, and they locked up the theater with him in it. We never knew what the truth was. Alta accused him of being with a woman, and they got into a nasty brawl and my dad was banished from the business. He stopped talking to Alta for almost the rest of the old man's life, until he was on his deathbed. After my dad was fired by Alta, we fell on hard times. He took a delivery job for Reddi-Whip, and things looked bleak for us until he went back to college on the G.I. Bill, and surprised us all by becoming a high school guidance counselor with enough credits to get his PhD. It made no sense at all.

"Remarkable," Dr. Myers said when I finished telling the story. "This Miami Beach experience is the central story of your analysis. It's a tent pole. It's the blueprint to your psychological formation."

Wow. We had a blueprint. A pole.

"You keep dreaming about Miami Beach because it was the real-life consummation of your deepest, most forbidden subconscious fantasy. It was in Miami Beach that you won the oedipal contest between you and your father."

"Oh yes?" I nodded expectantly.

"Your absent father was dead, killed by you and your grandfather when you were whisked away without your father's permission. In Miami Beach you had your mother to yourself for two weeks without your father. You even slept in the same bed with her. After watching her in bed with your father for so many years, it was your turn. But because your mother was a forbidden sexual object, your sexual confusion was crystallized."

My confusion was certainly crystallized. It sounded so . . . sordid. "Is that it? I mean, is that the blueprint?"

"There's something else that's significant. You said this trip to Miami Beach took place in March? Well, eight years later, on what might be the same day in March that you were in Miami Beach, you tried to kill yourself, the way Oedipus blinded himself."

It turned out he was right. I tried to kill myself on March 15, eight years to the day we left for Miami Beach. Spooky? Freud? *Bashert*?

The Miami Beach experience, he said, also explained the identity of the man was who was going to steal me away at school, or the stranger who was lurking in the men's room at the Culver. It was my father's ghost of vengeance. A child molester who would castrate me for sleeping with my mother, another reason why I turned away from women.

Really? It sounded fantastic, but it *did* tie up all the loose ends. Sort of. I liked the neatness of it. And anyway, I had less than a month to go before I was discharged, so I bought into this construction just to be practical.

Grand Rounds

Dr. Myers asked me if I wanted to be presented at Grand Rounds.

I was thrilled. I was a prince at the monster's ball. Being presented at Grand Rounds was like being nominated for an Oscar in the Academy of Mental Cases. I was so proud I told all the other patients as if I just had been notified I was class valedictorian. Only one person a month was chosen from the whole hospital, and it meant that there was a chance my case would be cited in a medical journal. You've heard of Freud's famous pseudonymous patients, "Anna O" and the "Wolfman"? I would be known as "Patient Miami Beach."

On the morning of my Grand Rounds I was escorted by an aide through a labyrinth of tunnels connecting Payne

Whitney with the main building of New York Hospital. Grand Rounds took place in an amphitheater, attended by medical students, interns, residents, professors of psychiatry. Bleachers of people in white lab coats filled the seats. The legendary chief psychiatrist at Payne Whitney, Dr. Oskar Diethelm, and the chairman of the psychiatry department, Dr. Eleanor Jacoby, sat in the first row of the gallery. I was shown to a chair on a platform opposite Dr. Myers, who smiled reassuringly. The entire room focused intensely on me, and it was so intense that I began to shake. It wasn't exactly as I hoped it would be. No cameras. No close-up. No Natalie Wood.

Dr. Myers gently put me through my paces, hitting all the plot points: my father's temper tantrums; sleeping in the same room with my parents; the trip to Miami Beach; how I hated my homosexuality; and that I wanted to change. I even cried for them, an Uncle Tom gay boy. Tears rolled down my cheeks as I expressed my torment at being homosexual and my longing to be like everyone else. I thought that if I could convince them, it would come true. Dr. Diethelm sat with his chin resting on his hand as I spoke, inscrutable, but Dr. Jacoby scowled.

When it was over, I felt exploited. Dr. Myers shook my hand and said, "Good job." Then an aide led me into the hallway behind the amphitheater to take me back to Payne Whitney when the door opened and it was Dr. Jacoby. She was smiling and she took my hand and patted it and asked if I was okay. She brushed my hair back from my forehead and said that I had been very brave, and that I was exceptionally articulate. Then she gave me a hug, and whispered in my ear, "Don't torture yourself."

Beekman Place

Richard Halliday graduated to the fourth floor about a month after I did and continued to ignore me. When I first saw him in the hallway I blurted out, "Hi, Mr. Halliday!" but his dour "Hello" rejoinder broke my heart. It was bitter medicine. I sometimes sat across from him at the same table in the dining room, stealing glances, but he would not look my way. I talked about it a great deal with Dr. Myers, and why Mr. Halliday's friendship meant so much to me. Dr. Myers suggested I try apologizing. So I walked up to Mr. Halliday one day and said, "I'm sorry if I did anything to offend you." Mr. Halliday looked at me and said, "Not at all," and continued to ignore me.

Then, toward the end of August, out of the clear blue, he stopped me in the hallway and asked if I wanted to be in a walk privilege group with him.

I nearly genuflected. Yes, yes, I assured him, and he said, "Then you better sign up!" I rushed to the nurses' station to sign for a place in his group, determined I was going to be the best walk privilege partner any psychiatric patient ever had. Since there was a minimum of three people in walk privilege groups, Halliday chose as a third a dour Belgian woman in her forties, whom I hardly knew, nor did Mr. Halliday, it seemed. I couldn't figure out why he chose her to be the third, or what we would all talk about during our stroll, until the three of us got to the corner of York Avenue and East 68th Street, where the Belgian lady peeled off without saying a word and disappeared up the street.

"Where is she going?" I asked, confused.

"I guess she's going to get laid," he shrugged. "In any

event, it's none of your business." He gave me a withering look. It was smotheringly hot and rivulets of sweat began to trickle down my neck and wet the back of my shirt. "Now, would you like to come to my apartment and visit with Mother?" he asked.

"But that's against the rules."

"I thought you'd like to spend some time with Mother," Mr. Halliday harrumphed, looking down the street for a taxi. "I guess I was mistaken."

"But what if they find out?"

"The only way they'll find out is if you tell them."

I had already cheated once with Mr. Kellogg when we went to the Plaza hotel, and didn't get caught. Maybe my complicity with Mr. Halliday would reinvigorate our friendship. So despite my misgivings, I agreed that going to his apartment would be a secret between us.

What followed was jarring. A Yellow cab took us to an apartment building in the Beekman Place area. The doorman seemed surprised to see Mr. Halliday, maybe even a little disturbed. "Is Mrs. Halliday out?" Mr. Halliday asked. The doorman said she had gone out, and Mr. Halliday barked, "Ring up when she comes home."

I didn't get it. He knew Mother wasn't home?

We rushed through a dark lobby into a wood-paneled elevator with a tufted bench to sit on. A uniformed elevator man took us up to a small landing with just one apartment door, painted a red enamel so shiny you could see yourself in it. Mr. Halliday led me to a large entrance foyer with a black-and-white marble checkerboard floor. There was striped silk wallpaper, and a curved staircase that led up to the bedroom floor. Ahead of us in the living room everything was lemony yellow, the rugs and walls and sofas and chairs, even the sunshine streaming in a row of tall casement windows overlooking the East River. Everywhere I looked there were exquisitely needlepointed pillows of every shape and size. The only dark object in the room was an immense black grand piano with the top down and dozens of photographs in sterling silver frames of Mother and Mr. Halliday posing with famous people. I was spellbound. I was in Mary Martin's house.

Halliday led me through the formal dining room into a big, dowdy kitchen that probably hadn't been updated since the building was built. It had putty-colored tiles on the walls, a six-burner gas range, and a worn porcelain sink so deep you could wash clothes in it. He told me to sit at the oilcloth-covered kitchen table while he rummaged around in the drawers. He put an opened bag of stale chocolate chip cookies in front of me, handed me a day-old newspaper to read, and ordered me to stay put. Then he hurried up a back staircase, taking the steps two at a time.

A few minutes went by while I tried to nibble on a cookie and browse through the newspaper when suddenly the kitchen door swung open and it was Mother! She was dressed in a navy blue suit with pearl buttons, and she didn't look any too happy to find me sitting at her kitchen table. I jumped to my feet, not knowing what to do. I guess the doorman forgot to ring up. "Where's Richard?" she scowled. She was really cross.

"I don't know," I said, petrified. "He told me to wait here."

She rushed off the way she came, the kitchen door flapping behind her.

Soon I heard angry stomping upstairs, and a minute later Mother came down the back stairs into the kitchen and said frostily, "Richard is waiting for you at the elevator." She turned her back on me and exited stage left. I never saw her fabled exit in *South Pacific*, but it couldn't have been any more effective or devastated anybody in the audience more than it did me that day in the apartment.

Mr. Halliday was waiting in the tiny vestibule, red in the face and stiff as a corpse. He didn't say a word to me in the taxi on the way back to Payne Whitney. I had sense enough to keep my mouth shut. By the time we got to York and 68th Street we were late, and the lady from Belgium was standing on the corner, hopping angry that we would be reported and lose walk privileges. She started to tell off Mr. Halliday, who gave her a look as though he would murder her if she said one more word, so she fumed in silence back to the hospital and up to the fourth floor, where they didn't even notice we were ten minutes late.

That night at dinner Mr. Halliday had no appetite. When one of the nurses asked him why he didn't eat his fish, he lashed out at her with such vitriol that everybody in the dining room stared at him. By the next morning his face was contorted in a rictus-like grin. While he was at breakfast they searched his room and found an assortment of amphetamines and barbiturates hidden in his clothing. Evidently when we went to his apartment he raided his secret stash of pills, hidden somewhere upstairs.

He told them he did it because he couldn't stand the August heat.

Dr. Myers came to the floor and confronted me about accompanying Mr. Halliday to his apartment. I cried, heartfelt heaving and sobbing, and begged not to be thrown out of the hospital for breaking the rule, because I had been duped by Mr. Halliday. Dr. Myers said he understood that I had been used as a pawn—after all, he had listened to hours of my adoration of Mr. Halliday and Mother. But rules were rules. I had to leave. However, instead of discharging me immediately, they decided that I should leave Payne Whitney in two weeks, at the end of August. The new plan was to mainline me back into the world of normal teenagers, and in September I would be enrolled in Erasmus Hall High School, as if I had never missed a day of school.

The Belgian woman was discharged from the hospital twenty-four hours later for going off on a *cinq à sept* with her inamorato, who was cheating on his wife. She pretended she was upset, but I think she was relieved to be getting out of there.

As for Richard Halliday, instead of discharging him, he faced a worse fate: they moved him up to the sixth floor. A nurse put all of his belongings on a gurney and as they walked him to the elevator a few people on the fourth floor came out of their rooms to say encouraging things like, "You'll be back down before you know it," and "We'll miss you."

Halliday nodded at them, stony faced, pale, and when he passed by me I said, "I'm sorry, Mr. Halliday," not certain what I was sorry about.

"Traitor," he whispered to me.

"Me? You're blaming me? I didn't tell them *anything*."

"Come along, Mr. Halliday," the nurse said, coaxing him into the elevator landing.

"*It wasn't me!*" I pleaded. "*It was probably Mother who told them.*"

The big oak door closed and it was done.

At Mr. Halliday's departure the entire fourth floor fell into a communal depression that was alleviated only by the arrival of an attractive thirty-two-year-old bachelor, the son of a congressman from Washington, DC, who was on the fourth floor for three days before he exposed himself and they sent him up to the sixth floor too.

Dr. Myers refused to tell me if Mother had phoned the hospital to tell them Mr. Halliday had turned up at their apartment. The truth was, nobody had to tell them, because it was pretty obvious from Mr. Halliday's demeanor when we got back to the hospital that he was on something.

I saw him one last time. The day before I was discharged I ran into him on the eighth-floor elevator landing. I was on my way to the occupational therapy room to get the ceramic ashtray I made (I thought it would be charming to have it on the coffee table later in life and say, "Oh this is the ashtray that I made when I was in Payne Whitney") when the elevator door opened to reveal Mr. Halliday and a group of patients standing inside. He was herded out of the elevator by the nurses, and I could see by the way he moved that he was on Thorazine. It was awful. He stared at me and I said, "Mr. Halliday, I wanted to say goodbye. I'm being discharged."

There was a blank pause, and then he said "Right," before a nurse led him away.

What did that mean, "Right"? Right meaning that he understood that I was leaving? Or that was I right? Did I do the right thing? Or did he say, "Write"? Did he mean that I should write to him? So I did, the following week after I was released, I wrote him three letters, one to the hospital address and two to his home, but they went unanswered and I had no idea if he ever received them. Then I decided that what he was really saying to me was not to write to him, but that I should write it all down. Write. Or did he?

On August 31 I packed my bags and, dressed in my Brooks penny loafers, chinos, and a madras shirt, I tearfully said goodbye to the nurses and patients. Dr. Myers was in the lobby to shake my hand. I climbed in the back of my dad's old Mercury and as we drove away I turned around to see the hospital building and all its secrets and characters disappear, and I whispered "Goodbye."

Six months later, when Wayne Myers finished his residency at Payne Whitney, he went into private practice and opened an office on East 75th Street off Madison Avenue, in a chic townhouse, where I went into full Freudian analysis with him. For most of the next twelve years I spent forty-five minutes, three or four days a week, lying on a black leather sofa that faced a framed print of Hieronymus Bosch's *Garden of Earthly Delights* hanging on the wall. I don't know how much the actual tab for all those years of trying to cure my homosexuality with Dr. Myers cost, but I do know that when my father asked, "Who's going to pay for this?" the answer was that *he* was going to pay for it. My mother and father made a great sacrifice hoping to cure their homosexual son. The doctor bills kept us poor, locked in the flat above the store, driving around in old cars, with no savings. To what end we were never certain.

Never-Never Land

One last thing.

When Richard Halliday left Payne Whitney he and Mother moved to a twelve-hundred-acre ranch in Brazil, where they grew coffee beans and raised chickens. To amuse themselves they opened a small needlepoint and gift shop in the local village. He died in Brasilia in 1973 at the age of sixty-seven from an intestinal blockage. Mary Martin sold the ranch and spent summers on Martha's Vineyard and winters in Rancho Mirage, California. In 1982 she was riding in a taxi in San Francisco when the cab was broadsided by a car running a red light. She never fully recovered, but it wasn't the accident that killed Mother, it was colorectal cancer at age seventy-six, in 1990.

Years after his death I discovered how detested Richard Halliday was in the Broadway theater. He was regarded as a monster, the vile side of his personality fed by amphetamines. Larry Hagman, Mary Martin's son from a previous marriage, hated him so much growing up that he fantasized about shooting him with a rifle from their Manhattan apartment window. Gossip says that Halliday was homosexual and Mary Martin a lesbian, but I saw none of that. Clearly, the love they had for their creation of Mary Martin-the-Broadway-Star transcended whatever their sexual preferences were.

Fifteen years after I left Payne Whitney I saw Mary Martin in a crowded Greenwich Village nightclub called the Bottom Line. It was a popular venue for record companies to debut talent, and Atlantic Records was holding some glittery premiere that night. Mary Martin was the guest of Ahmet Ertegun, the legendary founder of Atlantic Records, and his wife, Mica. People in the music business recognized the Erteguns, but I don't think another soul in the place knew or cared who Mary Martin was. I wended my way through the crush of people to where she sat and stood next to her chair. She looked up at me—she

was so different, an old woman, her eyes frosted over, her hair done, lipstick, a church lady—and words began to fall out of my mouth: *You probably won't remember me but I met you and your husband Richard when I was in the hospital*—I didn't say which one—*and you sent books for me to read, and knowing you and your husband helped set my life on a new tack .
. .*" I wanted to tell her about Richard saying I should write my family stories down and that I had become a writer and newspaper columnist, but I didn't get to tell her that part because Ahmet Ertegun was furious that I had intruded at his table and he was loudly demanding that I go away. Mary Martin, who probably heard only every other word I said in the din of the nightclub, smiled pleasantly at me and said, "That's nice."

Then the lights started to go down, and she looked away, and I went back to my table and took a seat in the dark.

Seven

4315 18th Avenue

I promise myself that I won't go back there anymore. Nostalgia is dangerous. I continue to try to remember my childhood so I can understand it better, yet I don't know what it is I'm trying to understand. Anyway, it's not as if something particularly astounding happened there. We were just another frayed thread in an infinite tapestry. Every family has its eccentricities and stories. It's only human to want to leave a mark. Every cabdriver thinks he should write a book. We all believe our lives are in some way special. We wouldn't be us if we didn't.

So against my better judgment, I occasionally drive to Brooklyn and park on 18th Avenue right in front of what was once Rose's Bras Girdles Sportswear, and I sit and I wait. And if I wait long enough, lulled into a stupor by the rhythmic rumble of the trains on the elevated line behind me, out of the corner of my eye I can see the specters *spazieren* down the street in ghostly cavalcade, my mom and dad, Muna, Gog and Katherine, the saleswomen waltzing with Old Man McGlynn in a top hat, the butcher, the baker, the candlestick maker, and me, round-faced, frightened, hopeful, somewhere in the middle.

The stage set of my youth has been disassembled. One autumn day in the 1970s old man Fleischman of the gown shop had a stroke, and his son with the pinky ring took over the store. Exactly as expected, the son gambled the money away on the ponies. The shop was padlocked and the creditors came and sold off the remaining stock of bridal and cocktail dresses for few dollars. Without Fleischman's foundation-garment referrals, the bread-and-butter trade of Rose's Bras Girdles Sportswear was all but over, and the store became dependent solely on Katherine's fashion taste. We tried to tell her the clothing she was buying wasn't going over on 18th Avenue, but she insisted she knew better. I think, looking back over her life, that buying the clothing for the store those last few years was the only creative thing she ever got to do, and she relished it. Right into the ground. Eventually Rose's Bras Girdles Sportswear ran out of money, and the store closed in the late 1970s, after a good run of over forty years.

The harpy salesgirl chorus dispersed. Lily Williams and her husband, Earl, moved to Palm Grove, Florida. Ten years later Earl died of a heart attack in his sleep, and Lily moved to an assisted living center, where she lived until she was ninety-one. Dodie moved to New Paltz, New York, where her son had a dental practice. Fat Anna became severely diabetic and rarely went out anymore.

My movie palace is gone too. The Culver Theater was sold to Chemical Bank and summarily demolished. Nobody noticed, nobody grieved. Only a few references to it on the Internet prove it ever existed. The secrets and intimacies the theater and I shared in the dark are now only mine.

I don't know what happened to my Culver Luncheonette antagonist Irv, but many years later I ran into Arnie. He had worked his way up in the food business from luncheonette owner to manager of a small restaurant on 10th Street in Greenwich Village. I was in a group of gay professional men going out for Sunday brunch, and when we came in the door he recognized me, grown up, and we smiled and shook hands. Then he asked us, "What can I do for you ladies?" Can you imagine? All those years later. We walked out.

A few weeks after that incident I remembered to relate the story to my mother, and she said that I must have seen him just before he died. She had heard from neighbors a few days before that Arnie had a heart attack while stuck in traffic on the Verrazano Narrows Bridge, and when the traffic jam eased up, they found him dead behind the wheel in the middle lane.

As for my grandparents, the delicate balance of Muna and Katherine and Gog was upset by a young woman named Carmela Carbone, of the pendulous breasts and heavy blue eye shadow. He was sixty-five, she was twenty-six. "You must understand this," he confided in me one day. "This isn't about money. This is love. Stevie, she's a gift to me."

"There's no fool like an old fool!" my grandmother shouted at him in front of all the salesgirls and customers. He had just told her was going to Miami Beach for a week, and she knew he was taking Carmela. "What does that *kurve* want with an old man except your bank account?" she shouted. Then she backhanded a dozen boxes of pastel-colored angora sweaters off the counter onto the floor.

Carmela knew what was in his bank account, because she worked at Merchants Marine Bank on 86th Street, where he did all his banking. Almost every day he found an excuse to see her, waiting on her line to make a deposit, trying to screw up the courage to engage her in conversation. Yet when he got up to the window he was so shy that he couldn't even hold her gaze. One afternoon he waited for her outside the bank, leaning on his cherry red fuel-injected Corvette to shore up his confidence. When she came out the front door he smiled and asked, "Miss Carbone, may I have the pleasure of your company for a cup of coffee?"

When my grandfather came home from Miami Beach tanned and sated, my grandmother could stand it no longer. First she had her hair done, a necessity of any self-respecting Jewish woman's commando tactics, and then she asked Fat Anna and her husband, Angelo, to drive her to Carmela's bank. Angelo double-parked outside in his beat-up Oldsmobile with the motor running, like a getaway car, while my grandmother and Fat Anna went inside. It was a big, old-fashioned bank with a high ceiling and chandelier, hushed, with long lines of customers. Rose spotted Carmela behind a teller's cage and marched up to her with Fat Anna hovering nearby protectively. "*Kurve! Kurve! Kurve!*" Rose shouted at Carmela. My grandmother's little voice bounced off the marble walls and the whole bank froze, like she had pulled out a gun. "You leave my husband alone!" she shouted. "He's old enough to be your grandfather!"

With that Carmela slammed down the gate of her teller's cage and came running out from behind the counter, heading toward my grandmother with her head down like a charging rhino. Just as she was about to reach her, Fat Anna hip-checked Carmela like a linebacker with all her 260 pounds. Carmela went down on the polished floor with the sound of flesh slapping marble. There were shouts and a scream and a guard came running. Anna took my grandmother's hand and together they hightailed it out of the bank and into the waiting car and sped off.

By the time they got back to the store, the police were there. It was a mess. Fat Anna and her husband and my grandmother had to go to the police station, where they were questioned for hours, until it was determined they had not tried to rob the bank. The bank agreed not to press charges, but they closed all of my grandfather's accounts and made him take his business to another bank. They didn't fire Carmela, but they transferred her to a different branch all the way in Queens, and she had to commute an hour to work every day. Of course, Gog was very angry with my grandmother. He said she had no right to bring her problems to Carmela's place of business and that he was disappointed in her. He sold the house in Freeport and my grandmother and Katherine were forced to move into the dreary apartment above the store where I had once lived. He moved in full-time with Carmela, but he still showed up at the store every morning to run the business as if nothing had changed.

Katherine died at age sixty-four, a suicide-by-cancer. She never gave up waging war against Carmela, holding out hope that one day Gog would return to her and my grandmother, and they would be whole again one last time. Then one day she came up with an ultimatum to get him back that she believed was foolproof. She found a lump in her left breast. She made my grandfather feel it and he pulled his hand away. He said she needed to go to a doctor at once, but Katherine said that she was going to let the disease take its course—unless he left Carmela and came back to her and Rose.

Gog teared up. He took Katherine's hand and promised her that he would stand by her if she was ill, come what may, and that he would pay for her medical care. But he would never abandon Carmela, because she was six months pregnant with his baby.

"Hah!" Rose laughed when she heard. "You don't have it left in you, old man, to make your *kurve* pregnant," she told him. "She probably got pregnant by a boyfriend that you don't know about. Wait until you see the baby comes out and it's black."

But it wasn't black. It was white and it looked just like Gog. They named the baby Anthony.

It was a bitter time. By the time Katherine agreed to have radiation, it didn't do much good. All her hair fell out and instead of buying a wig she wore a red wire wig from one of the store window mannequins. The night she passed away, in my old bedroom above the store, she was running a high fever, and the last thing she said was, "Harry, I'm burning up."

Perhaps the saddest thing about Katherine's death was that as important as she had been to our family—a mother superior to the children, my grandfather's paramour, my grandmother's best friend, the backbone of the retail business, a paragon of hard work—she wasn't Jewish and couldn't be buried with the family. She was laid to rest without ceremony in a Ukrainian cemetery somewhere in New Jersey, and no one ever went to visit her grave.

Rose hung in with Harry until the bitter end. When Gog and Carmela argued, and Carmela would throw the old man out, he'd temporarily go back to my grandmother, who always took him in. He was her man. She would wash his laundry in the kitchen sink, and make him baked apples, until a few days later he would abandon her again and go back to Carmela.

Every day for years, even in the winter, my grandmother sat on a folding chair in the street in front of the closed and bankrupt store. She chatted with former customers who passed by, and told the same jokes she had been telling since she opened the knitting store. She behaved as if she didn't realize the store behind her had closed. It was like the movie *The Swimmer*, with Burt Lancaster, based on a John Cheever story, about a man who swims home one Sunday using his neighbors' pools, not realizing . . . oh, never mind. My grandmother had always been happy with very little. She died at age eighty-four from a fall down the stairs, the same stairs I had counted up and down so many times. Maybe only a dozen people came to her funeral.

Gog died a year later, also eighty-four, of kidney failure. By then he was nearly broke trying to take care of Carmela and Anthony, who turned out to be a troubled kid. I called them once, after Gog died, to ask how they were doing, and when I told Anthony who I was, he screamed at me, "He was my father, not yours," and slammed the phone down. Anthony died in a police chase, driving a stolen car, when he was fifteen. Carmela still lives in Queens at the same address, all these years later, single. Maybe it was for real, Gog.

When my parents eventually left the flat above the

store, they moved to a one-bedroom apartment at the Sutton, a spanking new, fourteen-story, white-tiled apartment building on Ocean Parkway. The Sutton was posh for Brooklyn; it had doormen and a swimming pool out back. It was built on the crest of a terminal moraine, a hill of rock left by glaciers millions of years ago. It was one of the highest points in Brooklyn, and if the night was clear, on the horizon you could see the skyscrapers of Manhattan, to which I had fled.

The Sutton was built directly next to Washington Cemetery, a sprawling graveyard of mausoleums and headstones, a village of the dead that stretched out for miles, until it was cut off by the elevated line. My parents' kitchen and living room windows were directly over the cemetery, and they got to know the names on the tombstones like neighbors. The closest gravestone to their windows belonged to Marie Pollock, a person unknown to us except that she lived to be fifty-six years old, and the once brightly colored plastic flowers that someone had placed on her grave decades ago had turned brittle and white. When someone once asked my mother why anyone would want to live in an apartment overlooking the cemetery, she answered, "Because it's better to be living in the building looking down on the cemetery, than it is to be in the cemetery looking up at the building."

But not for her. I know you can't give anybody Lou Gehrig's disease, but the pressure of living with my father could have triggered it. Gog even told him so: "You made her sick." That was the end of it between them, him and Gog. Of their hundreds of bitter arguments, after "You made her sick" they never spoke again. She stopped speaking too, soon after. Her tongue went dead in her mouth and stopped moving, so she couldn't speak or swallow, a sensation that alone would have driven me mad, and then the muscles that inflated her lungs slowly stopped moving, and soon she was able only to blink. Every muscle in her body went flaccid. It was horrifying to watch. She turned into a human floppy doll, a pipe in her neck, a tube in her stomach, her bowels evacuated by a nurse in the mornings. My father emptied the dining room of their apartment in Brooklyn and turned it into an intensive care unit. Her care consumed him. Once she was on a respirator she needed twenty-four-hours-a-day nursing, and he hired a team to work in shifts. His insurance policy capped at $1 million, which was used up in about eighteen months, and my parents were forced into near destitution so my mother could qualify for Medicaid. The neighbors stopped coming by for visits; it was too disturbing for them to see her that way, and the nurses became my mother's only friends. They dressed her and cleaned her and took care of her and my dad as best they could. My father sat in the kitchen smoking cigarettes, a shell of himself, petrified of losing her. It went on like that for years.

On August 28, 1991, the day before their forty-ninth wedding anniversary, I went to see my parents in Brooklyn. I gave my mom a foot massage, I read to her from the paper, and we watched the news on TV together. I was as cheerful as I could muster, but I could see in her eyes she wanted me to go. I could see in her eyes that she wanted to go.

By the time I got back home, she was dead. My father had stepped out to mail a letter and when he returned five minutes later, she had suffered a cerebral hemorrhage, not unusual for people on a respirator. Yet I had a hunch. One of my mother's favorite nurses was with her, and it was possible to have accidentally jiggled the setting on the respirator so my mother would have had a painless, instantaneous death. I saw the nurse at the funeral. I looked her in the eye and thanked her, and called her an "angel," and we held hands and cried.

My dad was as mean as ever into his late seventies, but his heart was weak, and he was confused. I couldn't stand to see him that way, so no matter how much trouble he was going to be, I moved him in with me. After all, he was my father. We made peace, at least in my mind, the last few weeks of his life. There was one small moment. He had just finished breakfast, and he stood up from his chair too quickly and fell into a heap on the floor. He asked me to let him be for a minute, and I covered him with a blanket and sat next to him on the floor. We talked about the family and all the people who had died. When he got his breath back I lifted him off the floor in my arms—he only weighed 130 pounds by then—and as I carried him into his bedroom he surprised me by kissing me on the cheek. "Thank you for taking such good care of me," he said. Later that night he told me his sister had come to look for him.

The next day a health care aide and I tried to get him to take a bath, but he wasn't interested. "If you make me take a bath, you'll give me a heart attack, and then you'll be sorry," he warned. Those were his last words to me. Sure enough, as the aide and I lowered him into the bathtub, his heart stopped beating, he closed his eyes, and he slipped away.

Home, 4315 18th Avenue, was cleansed by fire. Literally. On September 11, 2013, a suspicious fire started in the hallway just outside the door to our old apartment, and the building burned to a charred shell. The police believe it was arson, but I knew better. It was *bashert*.

Expiation

For nearly ten years after I left Payne Whitney I was in psychoanalysis with Wayne Myers, trying to cure my homosexuality. I slept with women regularly, as prescribed, but took little joy in it. Since I approached the whole sexual thing as more of a tourist than a native, I became a connoisseur of the female body the way a Jew appreciates the Vatican. It was a matter of responsibility to be a satisfying partner, so I performed all the obligatory sexual acts, but without essential lust. And although I enjoyed the intimacy of sex with women, diligently pleasing a partner is not the same as making love. And making love is not the same as lust. Even psychiatry didn't claim to know how to make people lust. And lust is the glue of love. Oh yes it is. At least at first.

In my pursuit of love through sex, as the writer J. R. Ackerly put it, I would bed a woman for three or four months, and then wander off when things got too serious. Many of the women I dated were in search of a lifetime companion and progenitor and I felt like a cad; I was pretending to be earnest in my affections, when it was really a science project. There were women I loved, but not completely. No matter how wonderful the women I romanced were, I was driven by nature and design to love a man more.

It was of no help when in 1973 the American Psychiatric Association declared that homosexuality was no longer an illness. It infuriated me. I had a financial and emotional investment in being sick, even though I had come to the realization that it was foolish to go on trying to change it. I made an uneasy peace with myself. I understood that I had to stop trying to love women, and I had to stop trying to figure out why I couldn't, and I had to stop being ashamed of it. I realized that I had to get on with life, or I'd be left on the sidelines. I decided that my homosexuality might be a complication, but it didn't have to define my life, and I didn't have to be a professional homosexual. If I just let it be, I would be. I came out publicly at age twenty-six, when I published my first book, the biography of a child evangelist, Marjoe Gortner.

The gay world in the 1970s was shallow and unforgiving. Since we were outlaws, we had outlaw sex. Gay men were dissolute beyond belief. When I whined to my peers that liberation wasn't the same thing as promiscuity, I was told that I was a "bad homosexual." I was indeed. In any event, the intensely hedonistic world in New York had its appeal, and I tried to embrace that world, thinking it was all that was left me. How I missed getting the plague is a miracle.

I still do not feel entirely comfortable inside the gay world, despite its enormous strides toward equality. When I told a therapist that I didn't think gay men on the whole liked me, he said that was because on the whole, I didn't like gay men. I have none of the stereotypical talents ascribed to gay people. I can't arrange flowers, decorate houses, or cut hair, and I don't know or care what the best hotel is in Positano. And yet, if you asked me my blessings, chief among them was that I was born gay. And a Jew.

As for Wayne Myers, my analysis with him simply

drifted off as I moved into my late twenties and we lost touch. Thirty years went by before I saw Dr. Myers again. I was depressed, my worst depression ever, and my general practitioner suggested I pay Wayne Myers a visit for a catch-up. At first I resisted the idea, but he insisted I go see him. At the time Dr. Myers's office was on Sutton Place South, a share in a busy professional complex. One of the other psychiatrists ran group therapy sessions with recovering addicts, and it was a busy, noisy waiting room, not the chic, calm waiting room of Dr. Myers's office on East 75th Street.

When he opened the door, I was surprised to see the vibrant young psychiatrist gone, and an aging grandfather in his stead. He was, after all, in his seventies. Yet he had been such a powerful influence in my life, I remembered him only as a robust young man. He still had a crinkly smile and a wry sense of humor, and his eyes were still blue and kind. I was surprised because on the bookshelf behind him there were framed pictures of his wife and grown children, which would have been *verboten* by the hard-core Freudian analyst he had been four decades before. He even shared with me some thoughts about his own life, the pleasure he took in his hobby, photography, his pride in his career, his love for his family, and about growing old.

We caught up on my life. I was a successful author and journalist by then, with several national bestsellers under my belt. I split my time between the townhouse I had bought on West 11th Street in Greenwich Village, just like Herman Wouk's Youngblood Hawke, and a home near the beach in East Hampton, where I escaped to write. I had a few serious relationships, but I was single at the time. I told Dr. Myers that I was at peace with being gay, and it was no longer a consideration to me. He asked if I ever thought about the boy with the lawnmower and we laughed. I told him that I looked for the lawnmower boy all the time, and it's true. I know he's just around the corner, still a fresh-faced kid with his tee shirt stuffed into the back pocket of his jeans.

Toward the end of the session there was a long, clumsy silence while Dr. Myers tried to compose something in his head, and then, his voice full of emotion, he said, "I want to apologize."

"For what?" I asked nervously.

"I'm sorry I tried to change you. I'm afraid that, in retrospect, I caused you more pain."

I was breathless. *I didn't want him to be sorry.* To be sorry meant that all that effort was wrong. At the time we started therapy, being straight *was* the better of two worlds, and even if it failed, we tried. "Dr. Myers, there's no need to apologize," I assured him. "We were collaborators, trying to do what we thought would bring me happiness. It was about my happiness, ultimately. Wasn't it?"

He shook his head. "Part of the Hippocratic Oath is 'do no harm,'" he said.

"But I *wanted* it," I insisted. "Don't you see? Look, my analysis wasn't just about a cure. I had nothing when I met you in Payne Whitney. I had no way of *being* in this world. You were a father to me. You helped shape me into a human being. You taught me that integrity has its own rewards. About having an organized life. And you made me believe that if I really wanted to make something happen, I could. I never would have tried to write a book if it wasn't for you."

"I'm still sorry," he said.

I was so upset I didn't know what to do, so I did what was previously forbidden. I stood up and I walked to where he was sitting, like crossing an ocean of time for me, and I extended my hand. "Your apology is accepted, Dr. Myers," I said.

He stood up and we were eye to eye. He took my hand and shook it firmly. As far as I could remember the only other time we shook hands was the day I left Payne Whitney fifty years before.

I knew he still wasn't satisfied. He would never forgive himself.

He died six years later, in January 2009, from lung cancer, and it was only then that I found out anything about him, by reading his obituary in the *New York Times*. I sat at the kitchen counter and cried reading it. It turned out that the first day I met him at the hospital he looked so young because he was only thirty years old, just twice my age at the time. He grew up in Westchester, New York, graduated from the University of Arkansas, Phi Beta Kappa, and went to medical school at Columbia College of Physicians and Surgeons. His surgical residency was interrupted by the Korean War, where he became commander of the Fifteenth Medical Battalion, and he saved the lives of hundreds of men, supervising and operating on wounded soldiers in a Mobile Army Surgical Hospital under fire. After the war he decided to do a second residency in psychiatry, which brought him to Payne Whitney. In his later years he became clinical professor of psychiatry at Cornell Medical College, a supervising analyst at Columbia University's Center for Psychoanalytic Training and Research, and the author of five books. At Payne Whitney he was a senior resident, the fair-haired boy of the hospital.

It was fate that randomly assigned me to him toward the end of his psychiatric residency, shortly before he started a successful private practice, in which I was one of his first patients.

Perhaps the most surprising thing I learned about him by reading his obituary was that he was Jewish. All those hours I spent trying to explain my life to him from a Jewish point of view, and he never let on. I wonder to this day why he led me to believe he wasn't Jewish. I can hear him asking me, "And what would it mean to you if I was Jewish?"

A week after that last session with him, I received a bill for $300. Some things never change.